NAT KING COLE

There were sides of my husband, of course, that only a few people ever saw: the insecure Nat, the humorous Nat, the argumentative Nat. His stage performances were so polished, his musicianship so stylish, his lyrics so silken, his manners so impeccable and easygoing that his millions of admirers might find it difficult to picture a man who never, during his entire lifetime, quite accepted the fact that he was as famous as he was; a man who bit his nails and sometimes anguished over small decisions, a man who often held deep convictions beneath an outer layer of soft pliability, a man who loved private debate, who, while never vulgar yet had a complete command of profanity, and who, in almost everything, had a wonderful sense of humor.

NAT KING COLE

Maria Cole

A STAR BOOK
published by
the Paperback Division of
W. H. ALLEN & Co. Ltd

A Star Book
Published in 1982
by the Paperback Division of
W. H. Allen & Co. Ltd
A Howard and Wyndham Company
44 Hill Street, London W1X 8LB

First published in Great Britain by
W. H. Allen & Co. Ltd, 1972

Printed in Great Britain by
Hazell Watson & Viney Ltd, Aylesbury, Bucks

ISBN 0 352 31037 5

It is impossible to make a singular dedication of this book. It is therefore first of all for my children—Carol, Natalie, Kelly, Timolin and Casey—with whom my husband and I shared our love, and it is written in the hope that they will find something in my thoughts of their father that will help them to perhaps, in their own way, give to the world one-tenth of what he gave.

I would be far remiss if I did not also dedicate this book to Nat's legion of fans, without whose recognition and appreciation of the exceptional talent and qualities he possessed he would not have become the legend he is.

ACKNOWLEDGMENTS

There are many people without whose help and cooperation this book would not have been possible in its present content, but my love and special thanks go to my dear sister, Charlotte Sullivan, who was my husband's secretary for eight years; to Baldwin (Sparky) Tavares, Nat's valet, confidant and an all-round friend of the Cole family; to Nat's road manager of many years, Mort Ruby, who gave unselfishly of his own notes and remembrances; to Nurses K. C. (Casey) Bower, Viviane McKenzie and Joanne Andrisak, whose comfort meant so much to Nat and me both in the last months, and to the entire staff of St. John's Hospital for their complete cooperation, from the beginning to the end.

I am also grateful to Nat's and my close friends, Glenn Wallichs, Harold Plant, Hal Fein, Lee Gillette, Marvin Fisher, Ivan Mogull, Marvin Kane, Buddy Howe, Red Evans, Dick LaPalm and Sam Weiss for so generously sharing some of the warm memories of their long-standing friendship and association with my husband.

And last, but not least, there is Carlos Gastel, Nat's manager for many years, who, despite a lingering illness prior to his death, joined us in "Remembering" the man who is "Unforgettable."

*"The greatest thing you'll ever learn,
is just to love, and be loved in return."*

1

For me, the magic number was 1946—the year I met Nat King Cole.

It all happened as part of the chain reaction of the peculiar way in which lightning sometimes strikes our lives, transforming an ordinary existence into a miraculous wonderland beyond our most extravagant imagination.

To tie it all together, I have to go back in time for just a few moments to those events in my own childhood which led eventually to the life I had always really wanted.

By the time I was ten years old, I was filled with ideas that I would one day be rich, well-known, live in Hollywood on Sunset Boulevard, and be married to a famous man. I was dreaming, I suppose, the way any young girl dreams of the future, and included in that dream was the vision that I would someday become a singer. Formal vocal and piano lessons had already become a part of my upbringing, but they were not exactly the sort I had in mind. Indeed, I remember one of my singing teachers telling my family: "You might as well make up your mind that Maria isn't going to do anything but be a blues singer."

How right he was. At the age of twelve, wearing yellow overalls and pigtails, I hitchhiked from my home in Cambridge, Massachusetts, with two childhood friends—one who would become my drummer and the other my business manager—headed for New York and a chance on the then very popular Harlem Amateur Hour. Eight hours later, just outside Westerley, Rhode Island, we were picked up by a minister, who in turn was stopped by highway patrolmen who had seen us hitchhiking.

So ended my attempt for early stardom.

(In later years, however, I did go to New York and appeared on the same Harlem Amateur Hour and won.)

When it was finally time for me to go to college, after long winters of private boarding school, my aunt Lottie, who had headed the school, offered to send me to any college of my choice rather than have me stay in Boston with my father. But I balked, preferring to spend my morning hours at Boston Clerical College so that I could work at night with a local orchestra led by Sabby Lewis. His drummer's family were friends of ours, so he could chaperone me, picking me up for work each evening and bringing me home. Later, bandleader Blanche Calloway (Cab's sister) needed a summer replacement for four weeks one year. I was lucky enough to get the job, one of the singing experiences which helped make me more professional.

During my third year at Boston Clerical, there was another bandleader, Phil Edmond, who, when he needed a singer for a two-week gig in New York, offered the spot to me. I begged my father to let me accept, and he agreed, as he put it, "since it's just for two weeks," and I would stay with relatives in New York.

But when the two weeks were up, I went to work on my father again and persuaded him to let me stay in New York with my uncle Ed and aunt Rhoda, hoping for a show business career.

What came instead was a job arranged by Aunt Lottie with her friend, Dr. Mordecai Johnson, president of Howard University in Washington, D.C. I went to work for the school's purchasing agent, for at nineteen I was an excellent secretary, and the job was a good one.

After that came a wartime marriage which ended in tragedy, and now I was back in New York with a little band work behind me, including a short stint with Count Basie.

Two years before meeting Nat, I had been secretary to the executive secretary of the Harlem YMCA, but I was still hoping to make it as a singer.

One day my sister Charlotte gave some tapes of my voice to a friend of hers, Freddie Guy, who was a guitar player with Duke Ellington's orchestra.

The next thing I knew, I was looking up from my desk in the caged office, saying "Yes" to arranger Billy Strayhorn, whom Duke had sent over to offer me a job as the band's vocalist.

It was enough to turn the head of any twenty-year-old girl. For now I was truly a part of that wonderful world of fame and fortune to which New York could lay claim like no other city.

New York, where nearly twenty years before, famed dancer Florence Mills came home from an international tour and, gravely ill, stepped off the ship into the arms of a knowing mother who cried, "Baby, you've come home to die!"

New York, where A'Lelia Walker, the leading socialite of her era, had once held weekly salons at her town house on 136th Street, drawing together writers, poets, artists and musicians for drinks and conversation.

New York, where the society lions and lionesses who inhabited Striver's Row on West 139th Street between Seventh and Eight Avenues would later be moving on to the more lavish climes of Riverside Drive and West End Avenue in Manhattan, to Westchester, Long Island and Connecticut.

New York, where Lenox Avenue still burst into its orgasm of human joy on the night of a Joe Louis victory, where the name of Sugar Ray Robinson lit up the entrance of a half-dozen business places, where the great bands of Cab Calloway, Earl (Fatha) Hines, Jimmy Lunceford, Count Basie, Andy Kirk, Jay McShann and Lucky Millinder had seen some of their finest hours.

And in 1946 there I was with one of the greatest of them all, Duke Ellington, playing one of the greatest clubs of them all, the Club Zanzibar at Forty-ninth and Broadway. This was it! The Mills Brothers were there. So was Eddie (Rochester) Anderson, and Claude Hopkins' Band, and a great, gorgeous chorus line. So was a young vocalist named Maria Ellington, who Zanzibar owner Joe Howard said —as the comparison was made in those days—could become "another Lena Horne."

But I was a long way from becoming another Lena Horne. Lena had already become a motion picture and nightclub star, while my career was just beginning to move. My biggest claim to fame so far was working with Duke Ellington, whom I had just left (and to whom I was not related, as we kept having to explain), and I was doing my first act as a single, singing two songs per show on the Zanzibar bill.

(Actually, Duke had fired me as his vocalist after he discovered—as those things have a way of leaking out—that I was quietly planning to leave anyway. I never did learn how he found out.)

During our engagement at Club Zanzibar that August, the popular Mills Brothers started doubling at the Paramount Theater downtown. We were playing three shows a night then, not getting through until four in the morning, and soon the grind become too much for the Mills group. So the next thing I heard was that the King Cole Trio was coming in from California to replace them at the Zanzibar.

"Who's the King Cole Trio?" I asked.

"Oh, they're great!" I was told by Alice Bishop, one of the chorus girls who had known Nat from their school days in Chicago.

So the King Cole Trio came to town, on a day when the Zanzibar show was rehearsing. I happened to be at the mike singing when Nat came up backstage. He looked out and saw me from the back and said to a friend, Happy Robinson—as I found out later—"*Who* is *that?*"

"That's Maria Ellington," Happy told him. "She used to sing with Duke."

"Wow!" Nat replied. "If she looks as good from the front as she does behind. . . ."

That was Mr. Cole's earliest comment on his future wife.

Later he went and sat out front and I saw him for the very first time. He was sitting there in the thin, scattered audience of on-watchers, looking slightly sinister behind a pair of glasses.

When they introduced all of us later that day, I said,

"How do you do," and that was that. Or so I thought. Nat told me later that he would stand backstage every night and watch me. I did my numbers in a beautiful royal blue sequined gown, very tight and split up the front. One of the tunes I sang was Johnny Mercer's "Personality." It had been more or less choreographed for me and it went over great. My other number was "Come Rain or Come Shine." Nat couldn't stand it.

Whatever Nat's thoughts were at that time, I was still going my merry way. In fact, I guess I really tried to ignore him. I remember us passing one night backstage as I was coming off and he was going on. He looked at me and nodded. I said, "Oh!" and snubbed my nose up in the air.

I suppose I really should have been impressed. Almost everyone around was swooning over him, and even my sister Charlotte was a fan of his. Yet, when he started sending me champagne by his valet, I would send it back. I suppose I was very conscious of the fact that I was well brought up by a family that had not wanted me in show business in the first place. Although I loved and wanted the glamorous life, I never really got away from the attitudes with which I was reared. I thought Nat was like any other musician, just making a play.

So we really didn't speak for the first two weeks. The little exchanges backstage became simply a nod from him and maybe a little smile from me.

What brought Nat and me together was the Joe Louis-Billy Conn fight. It was their second meeting, set for June 19 at Yankee Stadium, and it was the talk of the town. Rochester told me that his wife, Mamie, was going to the fight, and I thought that was really something. Nat found out how excited I was about Mamie going and sent his valet in to ask me if I would like to go. My eyes popped and I blurted, "Why, yes!"

Nat had his opening.

"Rochester and I have to work," he told me, "but if you'd like to go with Mamie, I'll be happy to buy you a ticket."

So Nat gave me a $50 ringside ticket and I was just thrilled. After all, I was merely the girl singer on the bill, and this was a great deal of attention from the star of the show.

Not only did I accept his ticket and go to the fight with Mamie, but the next day, when Nat invited me to go with him and the Andersons to the races, I readily agreed.

Nat told me later that he had never been to a horse race before and couldn't have cared less about them; but when he saw I wanted to go, he was willing.

We held hands all during the races. I bet two dollars on a horse named Grey Falcon and won $40. In later years, when Nat and I were married, I never bet on anything but gray horses.

So now the courtship had begun, and it was aided greatly by the fact that I didn't get off work until four in the morning and had to take the subway home at that hour. Nat had a car and the trio was staying at 555 Edgecombe, so he asked me if he could drop me off. Now what girl couldn't accept a ride home at that hour?

Nat started taking me home every night, he and the other two members of the trio, Oscar Moore and Johnny Miller. I don't know whatever happened to poor Oscar and Johnny, but pretty soon it got to be just Nat taking me home.

Our relationship was still a very platonic affair from my point of view. For one thing, I had just learned something about Nat that neither of us had discussed. It first came up about five o'clock one morning after we had stopped to eat after the last show at the Zanzibar. It was a gorgeous morning with the sun coming up as we drove, and suddenly Gordon Jenkins' beautiful *Manhattan Towers* came over the radio.

Nat was innately a very bashful man. The suave, articulate romantic who glibly courted "Mona Lisa" and "Rambling Rose" was not the real Nat Cole. He was indeed very soft and gentle. People later often asked if Nat sang to me at home, and the answer was "very rarely." But he had a quality that came out in his work and that he was not able to express generally. If you pushed him it actually made him become even more introverted.

But that morning of the beautiful sunrise and magical music, we sat in the car and listened until the music ended, then Nat turned to me and said softly, "I'm in love with you, but you know I'm married."

This was what I had learned through friends a few days earlier. "Yes, I know," I answered.

"But I never met a girl like you before," Nat went on.

A few nights later, when he took me home, he kissed me on the cheek. Then he said, in a line that seems almost too corny to believe, "I guess you're going to slap my face."

I looked at him for a moment and answered, "No, I'm not."

Sure he was making a play, but he was so divinely gentle about it. It was hard to believe that there was such a man. I knew, of course, that I was not in love with him then. Still, his gentleness had begun to warm me.

Nat left town for three days after that, and it was while

he was gone that I realized I missed him and was beginning to care. It was a very strange feeling because of all the conflict with my upbringing. My sister Charlotte almost had a stroke, even though she did admire his singing. "A married man *and* a musician!" she wailed. "You've got to be kidding! I don't know what in the world is wrong with you!" I was beginning to get a pretty good idea of what was wrong with me. I was in love. When Nat wired me that he was coming back and to please meet him at the airport, I was there.

A few days later Nat was gone again, this time for about two weeks. Then he returned to New York to tape the Kraft Music Hall radio show. Our friend Happy picked me up and took me down to the studio where Nat was working.

"You know I'm only here for the day," Nat told me when I got there.

"Where are you going?" I asked, getting a sinking feeling.

"Indianapolis," he answered.

Then he made a gesture that everybody came to know later as a Nat Cole trademark—he brushed lightly under his chin with the back of his fingertips.

Finally he said, "Can you go?"

I had just closed my engagement at the Zanzibar, but actually it wouldn't have made any difference if I hadn't because at that moment I didn't care about the job or anything else.

"Yes," I told him, "I'll go."

A friend of ours, Ivan Mogull, who was also making the trip, didn't believe it. "Are you really going with Nat?" he asked me.

"I sure am."

"You don't have any clothes for the trip," he said, laughing.

"I don't care," I told him. "I'm going anyway."

"Go out and get her a toothbrush," Nat told Ivan.

He left, all three of us laughing.

When we got there, Nat sent me out shopping. I remember buying several outfits and two pairs of shoes. We stayed about a week.

Later I felt very guilty about it. First of all, he was still married. Secondly, even though I firmly believed that Nat loved me—and I knew now that I loved him—I was still a frightened young girl. I wasn't so dumb that I didn't realize he could just be playing around.

After we returned to New York we went for dinner one night at a Chinese restaurant across from the Club Zanzibar. Nat was eating steak and I was having lamb chops when suddenly he stopped eating to look up at me and ask, "If I can get my divorce, will you marry me?"

I was chewing at the time and all I could do was nod and gulp!

It was not as simple as that, however. Divorce itself is never a simple matter, and in the case of a man who was becoming as successful as Nat King Cole was, there are advisers, business associates, cronies and hangers-on to tell you what you should or should not do. There were certainly those who suspected that Nat had simply become enamored of some young girl and was going to give up his home and everything. There was a certain bandleader who telephoned Nat's manager, Carlos Gastel, long distance and urged him to come to New York because, as he put it, the situation was "serious."

Carlos came and talked to Nat, and at the end of their conversation he laid it on the line to him about what a divorce would mean under the community property laws of California, where Nat lived. "Do you love this woman sixty thousand dollars' worth?" Carlos asked.

"Yes, I do," Nat replied.

"Well, that's what it's going to cost you," Carlos warned him.

Nat's freedom from his first marriage took both time and money, but by the spring of 1948 we had our own wedding plans set. We would be married on Palm Sunday.

I was trying on my wedding dress at the shop one day when Nat stopped by with a long look on his face. "I've got bad news for you," he announced.

"What is it?" I asked with fear rising in my throat.

"We can't get married until Easter Sunday," Nat answered. "The divorce decree won't be final before then."

A one-week delay was certainly no disaster, but I just cried and cried. I don't know why.

2

Easter Sunday dawned cold and clear. By the time of the ceremony that afternoon, the sight around Abyssinian Baptist Church was amazing. Hundreds of persons filled the church and overflowed onto the sidewalks outside, while others leaned out the windows of nearby buildings.

I would have preferred getting married in a church of my own faith, the Episcopal Church, but this would have required special permission from the Bishop, since Nat was divorced, and would have taken longer than we wanted to wait. So, Nat being a Baptist, we had gone to Abyssinian, pastored by our friend Adam Clayton Powell, whose father was a friend of my aunt.

But Nat's fans couldn't have cared less about the place. The important thing to them was that it was the wedding of the King, the man who had given them "Straighten Up and Fly Right," "Sweet Lorraine," "It's Only a Paper Moon," "Route 66" and "The Christmas Song." And I was his Queen. No girl's dream of a storybook marriage was ever more romantically envisioned than the real one of mine.

Aunt Lottie still had not given her blessings to the wedding. Proud, New England-bred Aunt Lottie was Dr. Charlotte Hawkins Brown, a product of the public schools of Massachusetts and the Salem Normal School, with honorary degrees from such colleges as Wellesley and Radcliffe. Aunt Lottie, with whom my sisters and I had gone to live some years after the death of our mother, had founded the Palmer Memorial Institute in an abandoned church in a small town in North Carolina and had built it into a half-million-dollar institution, the first Negro finishing school in America. It was in this environment that, during school months, my two sisters and I learned, not only book education, but all those things that my aunt felt proper young ladies should know.

And here I was, traipsing up the aisle of a church other than my own to marry—of all things—a divorced musician.

I had chosen blue for my wedding gown because I didn't know that as a widow it was permissible for me to wear white again. Our wedding pictures later gave evidence to the fact that I obviously had not undergone enough fittings for the gown; it seemed to be falling off my shoulders. I carried a bouquet of white roses, which became a traditional gift from my husband throughout our marriage.

Adam performed the ceremony, which we all managed to get ready for only eight minutes behind schedule. Charlotte was my maid-of-honor. My bridesmaids included Elaine Fein; Pauline Miller, the wife of Nat's bass player; Duke's daughter-in-law, Evelyn Ellington; Laveda Lewis, a dear friend; Bill (Bojangles) Robinson's wife, Elaine, and my younger sister Carol, whose daughter Cookie was one of the flower girls. (My gift to my bridesmaids was a strand of pearls, and Ruth Poll, a very good friend of ours, gave me an exquisitely beautiful handkerchief that had been part of her daughter's trousseau at her own wedding, with all of the bridesmaids' names on it. I've kept it to give to my daughters.)

Our wedding reception following the ceremony was held downtown at the Belmont Plaza, at that time one of the posh hotels. Adam's wife, pianist Hazel Scott, was there, of course, as were Bojangles Robinson, Maxine Sullivan, Sarah Vaughn, and many other friends of ours in and out of the entertainment world. This was but the first of two receptions for Nat and me. The other was given by my aunt at home in Sedalia, North Carolina, where she invited quite a few of her prominent friends, then left town without attending herself! Although indignant about the marriage, she gave the reception only because it was the "proper" thing.

Newspapers and magazines later reported that our wedding was the largest in Harlem since May Robinson, a granddaughter of millionairess Madame C. J. Walker, was married in 1923 in a ceremony and reception that cost an estimated $45,000. I don't know about that wedding a quarter of a century before, but mine was surrounded by some rather interesting moments—like when I quit speaking to Nat thirty-six hours before the ceremony.

The trouble began when Nat and one of his ushers, Hal Fein, were supposed to pick up Hal's wife, Elaine, and me at the Taft Hotel at seven o'clock Friday evening. Instead, they went to a stag party for Nat and didn't show up until five o'clock Saturday morning. Elaine and I were livid! I was so angry at the wedding rehearsal that night, I wouldn't even walk down the aisle with the man I planned to spend the rest of my life with. A newspaper society editor had to stand in for me.

We didn't make up until the next night at dinner with Adam and Hazel at their home. I had never known what went on at stag parties before, and Nat nearly died when I found out.

The second blow came after Nat got a wee bit smashed at the wedding reception, as many a good bridegroom has been known to do. I didn't mind about the reception so much, but when we were alone that night, I dressed in a gorgeous nightgown that had been made for my trousseau. Later I asked Nat if he liked what I had worn our wedding night. He didn't remember a thing about it!

But if there was a humorous aspect to our wedding, there was also an undercurrent of tragedy. My sister Carol (we called her Babe), whose husband had died six months before, leaving her with three-year-old Cookie, was already desperately ill herself, although none of us realized it at the time. She was dying of tuberculosis, and a year later she would be gone.

Her death caused us much heartache, but she was to leave a legacy that would always be a vital part of our lives.

But on the day of our wedding, a year was forever away, and within twenty-four hours we were flying out of Newark for Mexico City. We checked into the hotel with six pieces of luggage, and two fur coats that I had brought because I was too uninformed to realize that I wouldn't get to wear them in that warm climate.

In Mexico, of course, we went sight-seeing to the usual places. We went to the bullfights, because nobody goes to Mexico without seeing them. Or, so we were given to understand. Well, it was my last *Olé*! Four bulls were slaughtered that afternoon, and I became almost sick to my stomach when one of them gored a horse. Nat, as unruffled as ever, was busy taking movies of the whole thing.

We had decided that part of our honeymoon should be spent on the beaches of Acapulco, even though neither of us was much of a swimmer. It was a bumpy hour and a half ride by plane from Mexico City and many of the passengers became ill, but we were so much in love we hardly noticed as we held hands and watched from the sky as a number of brush fires burned in the countryside.

Acapulco was still a sleepy little seaport in 1948, and we practically had the beaches to ourselves morning and afternoon. Of course we went like all visitors out to the high cliffs overlooking the Pacific, where Nat paid a diver ten pesos to leap into an ocean cove below. The Mexican divers seemed to be momentarily suspended in time and space as they executed their long, graceful arcs to the sea. Nat, of course, took pictures. Afterward we learned that an American had killed himself there recently, trying to make the dive. That afternoon, we got drenched by huge waves when we went motorboating out in the bay.

Even in this small Mexican city that had not become the tourist mecca it is today, I got a taste of my husband's growing fame. Autograph hunters besieged us, including musicians from the hotel's roof-garden orchestra. They all spoke English, which was good because our Spanish was limited to *buenos días* and counting to ten. I experienced some amusing moments because with my coloring and long black hair, I was often mistaken for Mexican by people who would come up to me and start a conversation in Spanish.

But all good things must come to an end, even the lazy enchantment of a honeymoon in Mexico. We spent our last hours in a forty-five-minute motorcar ride out to the suburbs of Mexico City and the famed floating gardens of Xochimilco. To celebrate our one-week anniversary, Nat bought me a corsage of gardenias from an Indian woman in a canoe, and for ten pesos an hour we floated along a willow-lined waterway in a canopied gondola named *Maria*.

3

The world could not have looked rosier than on that flight back from Mexico. Our lives loomed richly before us, and Nat had just received some marvelous news about a song of his—a song the origin and fate of which is a story in itself:

Being a successful singer has many wonderful rewards —and lots of little pains in the neck. Sometimes the two are so gently entwined that you cannot separate them, or guard against one without risking the other. The songwriters are a case in point.

Everybody is a songwriter; your aunt, your spouse's older brother and my sister. (My sister Charlotte actually did write, and one of her tunes, "To Whom It May Concern," became the title song in one of Nat's albums. She did the same thing for me in an album of mine, "Love Is a Special Feeling," and she also wrote "With You on My Mind," which Nat recorded.)

Because songwriters are so profuse in number, they inhabit all corners of the earth. At the Downbeat Club in Philadelphia one night, a member of the press sent his card over to Mort Ruby, Nat's road manager. Mort, who was busy at the time, had a waiter show the gentleman to a table and serve him whatever he wanted. When Mort was able to join the man a half hour later, in the expectation of giving him an interview, he was surprised to find that the newsman was not there to write about Nat, but instead had written a song he wanted him to sing.

In Oklahoma, a deputy sheriff pulled the King Cole Trio's speeding bus over to the side of the highway, and instead of handing out a traffic ticket, produced a song for Nat.

At the Paramount Theater in New York, one songwriter, in a burst of ingenuity, trapped Nat in the men's room and shoved a music manuscript under his nose with the joyful announcement, "Mr. Cole, I got a great song for you!"

Nat could only rejoin: "Please! Not here!"

And so it went.

Thus Mort Ruby was hardly in the mood to greet song-writers at 7 A.M. one morning backstage at the Million Dollar Theater in Los Angeles, having risen at an early hour to attend rehearsals and time the show after flying in from New York the night before.

As always in a theater on opening day, there is confusion: stagehands, lighting men, musicians trying to find their dressing rooms. It was in the midst of such a scene of turmoil that the doorman hailed Mort to tell him, "There's a goofy-looking guy back here. Wants to see Nat Cole's manager."

"I'm busy," Mort replied. "He'll have to wait, if he wants to. If not, whatever he has to say he can tell you and you can tell me."

A couple of minutes later the doorman was back to

Mort with a familiar phrase, "He's got a song he wrote for Nat."

"Aw, please," Mort replied. "Tell the guy to get lost."

But later that morning when Mort took a break, he was stopped at the stage door by a short young man with a shock of reddish-blond hair parted in the middle and tumbling down the sides. He wore a sweat shirt, dungarees and sandals, and he carried a soiled music sheet.

"I have a song I want you to present to Nat for me," he informed Mort.

"Who are you?" Mort demanded.

The young man mumbled the name Eden Ahbez.

"All right." Mort sighed resignedly. "I'll see what I can do for you."

After having his breakfast, Mort went to Nat's dressing room and tossed the manuscript on the table. "Here's another one to add to the collection," he declared.

"Hmmm, dirty, isn't it?" Nat said, eying it from a distance.

"Sure is," Mort agreed.

A few days went by and one night after the second show at the theater Nat summoned Mort to his dressing room and told him: "You know, Mort, you've been talking to me about doing a Jewish song. . . ."

"Yeah, I think it would be cute."

"Well, I think I've found one," Nat said, holding up the soiled music sheet Mort had brought him, and he began to sing the lyrics. When he finished, he turned to Mort and asked: "Well, what do you think?"

Mort pondered a moment. "I hardly know what to say, Nat," he answered finally. "It's Jewish-sounding, yes, but don't you think the lyric is a little far out?"

Nat tossed the music sheet back onto the table. "This could be a big thing," he mused. "Who knows?"

More days went by and meantime Eden Ahbez came back to the theater to see what had happened to his song. Unable to locate Mort, Ahbez talked to Nat's valet, whom he promised 50 percent of the tune if he could influence Nat to use it. It later turned out that Ahbez gave 50 percent of the song to almost anybody with whom he came in contact.

When the trio finished at the theater, they had some time off around Los Angeles, and Carlos Gastel went to talk with the two owners of the Beaucage, a little Sunset Strip nightclub located over a restaurant near the CBS Studios. The owners were brothers, one an accomplished musician who played symphony French horn, and the pair kept the club going with the financial help of a wealthy aunt. But the club nevertheless had fallen upon hard times, and a few of the performers booked there by Carlos had not been fully paid, including Mel Tormé and Peggy Lee. Carlos now sought to make a deal, taking over the club and relieving the brothers of the burden they had incurred.

As they sat in the club one night, working out the details, Carlos suddenly put his hands over his ears to shut out the sound of a woman furiously playing the piano and singing rather loudly. "What's that noise?" he asked above the roar.

"That's one of our acts," one of the brothers replied. "She's doing pretty good."

Carlos, now accustomed to the cool stylings and subtle tones of Nat King Cole, had less appreciation for the performer than did the other patrons of the club. "How much does she get?" he demanded.

"She's drawing scale," came the reply, "one hundred and twenty-five a week."

Carlos turned to Mort Ruby. "Write her a check and tell her to go home," he said.

Mort went over to the singer-pianist when she finished her set and told her quietly, "I'm very sorry, but we're changing the entertainment policy of the club. I'll make out a check for your last week's salary. How do you spell your name?"

"L-u-t-c-h-e-r," she told him. "Lutcher, Nellie."

Nat and the trio later began an engagement at the Beaucage, and on opening night at the second show three men sat at a ringside table. One of them was Irving Berlin. Nat knew that Berlin was in the house and he told Mort Ruby, "This would be a good time to break in that piece of Jewish material."

Mort agreed.

Nat finished his set with the song, and before he could return to his dressing room Berlin was already at the door. He rushed inside with Nat and offered to buy the song. "I can't sell it," Nat told him. "I don't know anything about it. I don't even know where the guy is who brought it to me."

Later, Nat said to Carlos and Mort: "Who owns this piece of material? Let's get hold of him so we can record it. We've got to get clearance."

While everybody scurried around to find the mysterious Eden Ahbez, Nat went ahead with a recording session for Capitol Records in Hollywood. Nat's sessions were something to behold. There was literally no rehearsal; Nat just told Oscar Moore and Johnny Miller what chords to play, and they had all worked together so long that they could anticipate each other. There was seldom more than one "take" on a tune.

This particular day, Nat got the okay sign from the control booth to begin, played a little introduction and began to sing the lyric. Two minutes and forty-five seconds later he finished, looked up and listened for the reaction of the men in the control booth. No sound came.

"What's the matter?" Nat yelled out. "Was it a bad take?"

Still no answer.

"Jim! Do you hear me?" Nat called out to Jim Conkling, the man in charge of the recording session.

Jim leaned against the glass window of the control booth and motioned for Nat to come inside.

"Where in the world did you get that piece of material?" he asked as Nat entered.

"Mort got it from some goofy-looking guy while we were playing the Million Dollar Theater," Nat told him.

Then Nat and Mort explained the whole story to Jim.

"We have got to find this guy," Jim said. "Unless I miss my guess, this will be the biggest piece of subtle material I've ever heard of. Mort, find the guy and make it fast!"

Mort took over an office at Capitol Records and the search began in earnest. Calls went to the musicians' union and song publishing firms without success. Finally, Mort turned up a lead: Eden Ahbez had been hanging around Sunset and Vine, and was apparently a practicing yogi who lived out of a sleeping bag somewhere up in the Hollywood Hills. Mort checked with the police, who advised him to look under one of the L's in the big HOLLYWOOD sign on the hillside.

Sure enough, Mort found his man under the first L.

Ahbez didn't really recognize Mort until he mentioned the name Nat Cole, then the two of them went off to make a business deal.

But the little Jewish song was to lie silent a while longer. Capitol executives had decided the lyric was too subtle for the record-buying public's taste.

Months went by, and Nat was back in New York where a recording date had been set up for some Pete Rugolo arrangements. Nat liked a song called "Lost April," which had been used briefly for musical background in a motion picture called *The Bishop's Wife*, starring Cary Grant, Loretta Young and David Niven. Now Pete had written the song up for a big band with strings to accompany Nat, and it was beautiful.

When Nat finished up the scheduled recordings with time to spare, it was suddenly decided to try the Jewish tune with the strings and full orchestra treatment. Pete quickly explained to the musicians what he needed in the way of an introduction and other effects, and the song was done as a last-minute addition to the session.

Two days later Jim Conkling telephoned Nat to tell him how great the whole session sounded, and that everyone thought "Lost April" had tremendous possibilities to become a hit. Capitol was going to back it up, he said, with the little Jewish tune.

"Lost April" was indeed very pretty, but it was the flip side that sold over one million copies. They wired us on our honeymoon in Mexico to give us the good news that Nat's gentle, sensitive rendition was the biggest musical hit in the country.

The song was "Nature Boy."

At the end of 1947 a rumor had spread through the

record industry to the effect that Nat Cole had made a recording that would be one of the greatest in history, but no one had heard it.

In March of 1948, a copy of "Nature Boy" was delivered to music librarian Al Trilling at New York radio station WNEW. Trilling played it through once and rushed it in to disc jockey Jerry Marshall. Jerry put it on and before listening to it all the way through made up his mind.

At 2:16 P.M. on March 22, Jerry introduced the new tune on the station's Music Hall program with the prediction: "Here's a winner—a song everybody is going to love."

By 2:20 P.M., the station was swamped with calls.

During the first few weeks, the song was played at least ten times a day on the station. "People were mad for it," Al Trilling recalled later. "After every airing, we would get twenty-five or thirty phone calls."

In the music business since 1923, Trilling felt "Nature Boy" was one of the most beautiful songs ever written. "It's almost a tone poem," he explained. "The words and music answer the longing in everyone's heart."

People saw the closing line of the haunting melody—"The greatest thing you'll ever learn is just to love, and be loved in return"—as the answer to the world's quest for peace and happiness.

Making the song even more unique was its construction, which was simple in the extreme. It consisted of exactly eight lines of lyrics and sixteen bars of music, about half a chorus long.

Others later recorded it: Frank Sinatra, Sarah Vaughan, Dick Haymes. But only in the voice of Nat King Cole did it so completely touch so many heartstrings.

4

There was much I was to learn about the man I had married; and much that the world was to learn. Although he had already achieved a great measure of fame as a jazz pianist and singer, Nat Cole had not yet become one of the foremost entertainers of the American stage, and one of the best-known men in the world. (As a national magazine was to say later at the time of his passing, ". . . he was the most celebrated Negro to die in world history.")

The man the world was later to know as Nat King Cole was born Nathaniel Adams Coles on March 17, 1919, in Montgomery, Alabama, the second son of a Baptist minister, the Reverend Edward James Coles, and his wife, Perlina.

In all, there were six children and the whole family seemed to show musical talent from the very start. Nat's mother was the only piano teacher he ever had, as he was to say later with pride, but her hope was that he would become a classical pianist. Thus, his first public appearance came at the age of four on the stage of the Regal Theater in Chicago, where the family had by then moved. It was during a talent contest, and Nat's older brother, Eddie, had to literally push him on stage, where the small, frightened boy half sat and half stood as he played his masterpiece, "Yes, We Have No Bananas." Probably to his own amazement, he won first prize—a turkey.

But there would not be many professional "turkeys" in the life of Nat King Cole.

Nat's early display of musical talent was being put to steady use by the time he reached kindergarten, where he played piano while the children marched about during their games. During this tender age, little Nat was already evidencing the natural curiosity he maintained all his life about a lot of things: politics, sports and the like. Then, however, it was certain aspects of religion that aroused his curiosity. His father was lecturing on the all-powerful abilities of God one Sunday morning, and stated in no uncertain terms that God could, in fact, do anything. When the family returned home after the sermon, Nat watched his mother preparing dinner over a coal stove. Soon his eyes were traveling from his mother to the red-hot coals to his father and back again. Reverend Coles, fearful that the child might touch the stove, watched him carefully. But Nat had no thought of touching the stove. Instead, he was thinking of his father's words in church, and finally he said, "Dad, you said God could do anything?"

"Yes, God can do anything, son," Reverend Coles replied.

"Well," said the small boy, "I bet He couldn't get bare naked and sit on this red-hot stove with no clothes on!"

It was evident that even then Nat had his own ideas about things. He made this even clearer a short time later when he came home from school one day and asked for canned goods to take back to the "poor children." His mother, somewhat surprised at her son's lack of realization of the low finances of the Coles family, exclaimed: "Why, you're poor yourself."

"Mama, are we poor, sure-nuff poor?" he asked.

"Yes, we're poor," his mother assured.

"Are we poor, poor, poor?" Nat demanded.

"Yes, we are!" Mrs. Coles said.

"Well, Mama, one day my name will be up in lights and we won't be poor anymore," Nat told her. Long after that, at the Riverside Theater in Milwaukee, Mrs. Coles would look up at the marquee and see her son's name and remember his words.

It was inevitable, of course, that young Nathaniel, as a minister's son, would have to pay his dues in church. At the age of eleven, he joined his sister in playing piano at his father's True Light Baptist Church. He played the gospel songs while Evelyn played the slower numbers.

But church songs were not enough to satisfy Nat's insatiable musical appetite, and by the time he was sixteen he formed his own musical group, called the Royal Dukes. The band played for quarters, half dollars and, when they couldn't get cash, often settled for hot dogs and hamburgers. Nat wanted to sing even then, but the boys in his band listened once, decided he had a terrible voice, and that was that. Later, when his brother Eddie put together a group called the Rogues of Rhythm, Nat played with them. The pay was great—eighteen bucks a week—and when you're a teenage boy afire with music, it's easy enough to work until two A.M. and still arise early for classes. Nat attended Wendell Phillips High School, where he showed both a fondness and talent for sports.

The arrangement did not sit so well with the boys' father,

however. In later years, Nat remarked, "It was a long time before my own father reconciled himself to my singing jazz, but he finally got used to it."

The Rogues of Rhythm were good enough musicians to travel, although not always good enough businessmen to be sure of the soundness of their journeys. Once during a Southern tour, the group ended up broke and sitting on their instrument cases in Jackson, Tennessee. They were stranded there for about two weeks before they managed to convince a bus driver to give them a ride home to Chicago. He held their instruments as security.

Eddie, Nat and the Rogues eventually joined a revue called *Shuffle Along*. It was while playing piano in the revue that Nat, who was then only seventeen years old, met dancer Nadine Robinson, whom he later married.

When *Shuffle Along* got ready to shuffle westward six weeks after the Rogues joined, leader Eddie Coles chose to stay behind. Nat Coles chose to go. The two brothers fought in the snow over the issue one morning, but Nat went anyway.

Nat and Nadine were married as the show moved west, but a short while afterwards, *Shuffle Along* folded in Long Beach, California. For a while during the lean year of 1937, Nat played piano in what he later remembered as "every beer joint in Los Angeles."

It was in just one such beer joint on Santa Monica Boulevard that a club owner named Bob Lewis heard Nat play. Bob was fascinated by the piano artistry of the then unknown performer, and offered Nat a job at his club, the Swanee Inn on North La Brea. The club's principal talent around that time consisted of singing waiters, but Lewis suggested that Nat put together a small musical combo. "Can you get three other musicians?" Lewis asked. "Maybe a bass, guitar and drums."

The next day Nat went down to the Negro Musicians' Union and talked with Wesley Prince, a bass player, Oscar Moore, who played guitar, and drummer Lee Young. They all agreed to an afternoon audition at the Swanee Inn, except for Lee, who, having just purchased a set of new drums, had his heart set on joining a big band rather than playing with a small group.

Thus, the Nat Cole Swingsters Three was born. Had Lee Young made it, the group that was eventually to be known as the King Cole Trio would have been a quartet. Lee later played on all the trio's recordings, however, and in later years was Nat's musical director.

It was Bob Lewis, a man with a flair for showmanship, who decided that Nathaniel Adams Coles should be Nat King Cole, and he went out and bought a little red crown which he placed on Nat's head one night to signify the beginning of his royal reign.

The original Nat King Cole Trio was in business, earning twenty-five dollars a week each, with club owner Lewis occasionally slipping Nat an extra five or ten dollars.

The group might have remained strictly instrumental had it not been for a persistent bar customer—forever nameless—who wouldn't take no for an answer.

There is an oft-told story of how my husband became a singer. It involves a tipsy regular patron of the Swanee Inn who showed up one night, as usual, and demanded that Nat sing "Sweet Lorraine." Despite Nat's protests that he did not know the song, and with the encouragement of owner Lewis to keep a customer happy, Nat Cole reluctantly sang "Sweet Lorraine," and thus a singing star was born. That's the way the story goes.

A slightly different version of it makes the customer a female lush, who even went so far in her insistence to have Nat sing a song he didn't know that she left the bar temporarily, returned with sheet music in hand, and plopped it on the piano in front of him.

Over the years, the truth of how my husband became a singer is so entertwined with legend that it is now difficult to separate the two. Nat once explained that the story "sounded good, so I just let it ride." But when he had occasion to recall the beginning himself, as he did in a radio interview with Dick Strout, he told it this way: "When I organized the King Cole Trio back in 1937, we were strictly what you would call an instrumental group. To break the monotony, I would sing a few songs here and there between the playing. I sang things I had known over the years. I wasn't trying to give it any special treatment, just singing. I noticed thereafter people started requesting more singing, and it was just one of those things."

Yet the incident of the insistent barroom customer, a guy who often spent as much as "three bucks a night" in the Swanee Inn, did happen. As Nat explained it, "This particular customer kept insisting on a certain song, and I told him I didn't know that one but I would sing something in place of it, and that was 'Sweet Lorraine.' "

The trio was tipped fifteen cents—a nickel apiece—for that performance, and the customer requested a second tune. Again, Nat didn't know it but asked, "Is there something else you would like?"

"Yeah," the customer said, "I'd like my fifteen cents back."

Since this one customer was given virtually complete credit for the birth of Nat King Cole the singer as the legend grew, it was turned into a publicity gimmick years later when, on a radio show called *We, the People*, Nat offered a thousand dollars to find the man, but he never came forward.

The early days of the trio were not one magic carpet to success, however. As my husband later recalled, "When we started out, we had no one to copy from. Trios were unheard of then. The big bands were popular and agents used to laugh at us. 'Three men,' they would say, 'why, you don't fill the stage. If you get some more musicians, perhaps we can use you.' Because of our small combo of piano, guitar and bass, agents used to tag us the 'Chamber Music Boys.' "

Even Nat must have sometimes had his doubts. Although they became a minor sensation around Los Angeles, they still did not set the rest of the nation on fire with their first cross-country tour. Still, Nat clung stubbornly to his small-combo idea. When someone at the Club Alabam spied him sauntering along in a drizzle at two A.M. and called, "Come on in out of the rain, Nat," he answered dejectedly, "I ain't got enough sense to."

One of Nat's earliest and perhaps most fortunate business relationships began one morning back in 1942, when he called a friend, Carlos Gastel, and asked him if he could drop by the 331 Club where the trio was playing that evening. Meanwhile he wanted Carlos to think of someone who would possibly make a good manager for the group.

Nat had once asked Carlos himself about taking on the job, but Carlos had declined. Born in Honduras, Central

America, Carlos had attended school in San Diego and at the University of California at Los Angeles. It was while attending UCLA and listening to radio music that Carlos became interested in jazz.

He first met Nat at the Fox Hills Cocktail Lounge on Pico Blvd. in Los Angeles in the late thirties, shortly after leaving UCLA. Carlos admired Nat's work and soon he and his friends were visiting whatever spot in Los Angeles that the Nat King Cole Trio happened to be playing. Meanwhile, Carlos began his own career as a personal manager in the entertainment field by picking a couple of bands headed by Sonny Dunham and Stan Kenton. Neither of the orchestras was making any money to speak of, and, to the fledgling manager, the Nat Cole Trio would have just meant a third financially defunct client.

But as Carlos drove down to the 331 Club that evening with his sister Chickie, he discussed Nat's management problem. "You've got two headaches now," his sister ventured, "so a third one will go right along with the other two. You're around with them in all your spare time anyway and you feel they have such a good future, I just think you're crazy if you don't manage Nat."

When they reached the club, Nat asked Carlos, "Well, did you think of anybody?"

"How about me?" Carlos said.

"Would you still consider it?" Nat replied, brightening up. "That's what we would like most if you could do it. That is if it wouldn't be too much of a hardship on you."

"Yeah, Chickie's been talking to me and I think we could do something," Carlos told him.

"Well, that would be wonderful," Nat replied.

The next day, Nat and Carlos were on their way to see a lawyer about drawing up an agreement between the two of them when they stopped at a drive-in for lunch.

"Listen, there's no sense in paying me anything now," Carlos started to explain to Nat, "because you're not making enough money. It's better for you and me and everybody else in the long run if you take that money you would be paying me—although I could sure as hell use it—to build something up."

Nat thought a moment. "No, I want to pay you right off the bat," he said finally.

"Well, that's kind of silly," Carlos insisted.

"No, it isn't silly," Nat told him, "and I'm not being overly kind to you. It's just that I want you to get paid so you'll do something. If you're not getting paid, the chances are you won't pay as much attention to us as you should."

The two compromised on a deal whereby Carlos would receive no money until the trio was earning at least $800 a week, then he would make his commission. Nat felt this arrangement was completely unfair to Carlos, but the third week of their partnership the trio hit the $800 mark at the Orpheum Theater in Los Angeles. Said Carlos later, "We would have gotten five thousand if I had known what we were worth."

Even so, the $800 a week at the Orpheum represented quite an increase over what the trio had been earning three weeks earlier, when the three of them were splitting $225 each week. It was an equal three-way split. They would get paid each Friday night and when the money was presented to Nat, he would then count out a third for each of them, minus social security deductions. Then they would go their separate ways, not to meet again until show time when Oscar and Johnny Miller (a replacement for Wesley Prince, who had gone into military service) would come in, open up their instrument cases and start playing. At 2 A.M., they would stop, put their guitar and bass away and go home. But it was Nat who had been handling all of the business details: getting bookings, talking with club owners, doing promotion, and at the same time trying to create things musically, (Not that Oscar, certainly, did not make his creative contributions. He was a wonderful musician.)

Later, when Nat really started singing, it was obvious that in addition to his being the leader, he was the big moneymaker. Meanwhile, Carlos arranged for all expenses to be deducted from earnings first, then Nat received 50 percent of the remainder, with the final 50 percent being split 60-40 between Oscar and Johnny. Even so, when Nat's fame as a singer began to spread, there were weeks when Oscar was earning as much as $1,600 to $1,800.

5

In Hollywood in the spring of 1942, a new recording firm was formed by three men: record-store owner Glenn Wallichs, songwriter Johnny Mercer and movie producer Buddy DeSylva. The cash, some $10,000, came from Buddy. Glenn was business manager and Johnny handled artists and repertoire.

The new company had come about as a result of talks between Glenn, who thought selling and distribution techniques of the large recording houses were outdated, and Johnny, who felt there were too many poor arrangements, technically irregular recordings and general mishandling of talent in the business.

They could hardly have picked a worse time to start a record company. There was a wartime lack of shellac for cutting new discs. So the company bought old records at six cents a pound and ground them up to make twenty thousand records a week. With Johnny Mercer writing a couple of hit tunes and Buddy putting in another $15,000, the company managed to survive, despite the fact that on

August 1 of their initial year, James C. Petrillo, then czar of the National Musicians Union, barred all musicians from making new records.

Still, Capitol, in its infancy, found itself a sales firm without adequate supply.

But Glenn remembered the lean young piano player whom he had met back in 1940 when he opened his shop, Music City, which became a rendezvous for musicians. Nat's trio had been playing down the street at the Radio Room, a bowling alley barroom, for about sixty dollars a week. Nat came to play at the Music City opening and he and Glenn had become friends. During the thirteen months of the Petrillo ban, Glenn bought the master recording of "All for You," which Nat had done for a small, obscure label. For the first year of its existence, the company had little else to offer.

By October of 1943, however, the ban was lifted and the Nat King Cole Trio recorded "Straighten Up and Fly Right," an improbable little tune about a monkey and a buzzard and a ride in the air. Nat took the title from his memory of one of his father's church sermons, and had sold the song for fifty dollars' worth of room rent back in 1937. (The latter was a mistake, for "Straighten Up and Fly Right" became a war-time hit. Furthermore, the song eventually netted its publisher some $25,000.)

Nat Cole was suddenly in demand, and filled that demand with "Sweet Lorraine," "It's Only a Paper Moon" and "Route 66." But despite the sudden emergence of the Nat Cole voice, he was still first considered one of the foremost jazz pianists of his time. It was also during those still-lean, early forties that the names Aye Guy and Shorty Nadine began to show up as pianist on a series of Jazz at the Philharmonic recordings. If you listened closely, you discovered that those two sounded an awful lot like Nat Cole.

But Nat's impeccable taste and vocal styling, of course, soon established him not only as one of the leading crooners of the day, but also as one of the best song salesmen in the business. He could take the most unlikely lyric and transform it to a hum or whistle on everybody's lips. (For example, Lee Young later admitted, "We laughed when he did 'Nature Boy.' We thought 'Mona Lisa' was a joke.")

With "Mona Lisa" and "Too Young" added to the million-seller list of 1951, Capitol Records, no longer little more than a storefront operation, was selling Nat Cole records as fast as it could wax them.

The commercial success of the King Cole Trio and the increasing demand for the vocalizations of its leader was not going unnoticed by the trio's loyal jazz aficionados, however. Soon some began to express their concern and, gradually, to look accusingly at Nat.

One night *Metronome* magazine editor Barry Ulanov dropped by the Trocadero nightclub in Los Angeles where the trio was appearing, and Barry came right out and asked Nat why he was playing so much pop and less jazz.

A few nights later at a party, jazz writer Frank Stacy approached Nat with the same question. The two of them didn't really get into a discussion of it there, but agreed to meet soon thereafter for a breakfast-luncheon talk at the Radio Room, a Hollywood and Vine hangout for music industry people.

It was apparent from the moment Nat began talking that he was getting hot under the collar from the persistent jazz-vs.-pop question.

"I know a lot of you critics think I've been fluffing off jazz," Nat told Stacy, "but I don't think you've been looking at the problem correctly. I'm even more interested in it now that I ever was. And the trio is going to play plenty of it. Don't you guys think I ever get sick of playing those dog tunes every night?"

"Sure," Stacy answered, "but why do you keep on playing them?"

"I'll tell you why," Nat said instantly. "Frank, you know how long it took the trio to reach a point where we started making a little money and found a little success. For years, we did nothing but play for musicians and other hip people. And while we played that way, we barely got along financially. We practically starved to death. When we did click, it wasn't on the strength of the good jazz that we played, either. We clicked with pop songs, pretty ballads and novelty stuff. You know that. Wouldn't we have been crazy if we had turned right around after getting a break and started playing pure jazz again? We would have lost the crowd right away."

Stacy found it hard to argue with that logic.

But Nat wasn't through. "Like I said, don't think we're fluffing off jazz. We're only waiting until we reach a firm enough point where we can start mixing the real stuff in with the popular and still have an audience. And I think we're just about at that point now. I'm already planning to make more and more jazz records. Maybe every second side will be straight jazz from now on. In fact, we have a jazz side out right now on Capitol, 'Sweet Georgia Brown.' There'll be lots more of it. Don't you guys see that now we can begin to put down some real music and still get people to listen to it?"

Nat then revealed to Stacy his plans for a nationwide concert tour featuring jazz music, including some original material he was then writing, for the coming year.

"That's good news," Stacy told him.

"I didn't want to say anything about it for a while yet," Nat confided, "but I know how many critics have been shouting that Nat Cole's trio has gone the way of all commercial flesh, and I don't like to hear that kind of talk."

Nat had no way of knowing then that fate had stacked the cards against his best intentions. But God had given him a greater talent, and God would see that he used it.

In 1951, Nat announced that he was abandoning the trio, a group which one national magazine called "the greatest instrumental combo of all times." Guitarist Irving Ashby, who had by then replaced Oscar Moore, left the group declaring, "The truth is that any one who puts in a year or so of study on the guitar could play all the guitar that Nat needs for the kind of music he's playing today."

Nat's bass player, who by then was Joe Comfort, added his thoughts on Nat's jazz-to-pop musical evolution. "I guess I just set my hopes too high," Joe said. "Nat knows what he wants to do. Maybe he's right, but it's not for me."

It was very much right for Nat, however. As he pointed out: "During the last seven years I've made most of my recordings with big bands. These recordings were my biggest sellers. So, I decided it was time to step out as a single attraction. I am trying to broaden my field, to please a majority of the public."

In another three years, Capitol was doing $20 million worth of business, with Nat's annual gross record sales averaging out to nearly $2,500,000. Four of the company's ten all-time best sellers were Nat's. "He is our most consistent solo artist, among perhaps twenty we have under contract," Glenn Wallichs said proudly. "All the publishers offer us a tune for him first, because they know if Cole sings it, they have an eighty to twenty chance of having a hit."

And my husband, through the wonderful instrument of his voice, was becoming an American institution.

6

The transition from a piano player who sang to what critics later called "the master balladeer" was not necessarily swift for my husband. But as that hoarse, clean enunciation that marked his voice became more and more matched with new soft lyrics that seemed made for him, the change began.

It had started shortly after two young men named Mel Tormé and Bob Wells wrote "The Christmas Song." They came into the Trocadero, where the trio was appearing, late one night at closing time, and wanted to know if he would have time to look over their tune.

"This is a very pretty song," Nat said after looking it over, "but it's no good for a trio. This needs a full band for a big background. But it's a beautiful thing and I wish I could do it, if I had a different kind of instrumentation."

Carlos Gastel was there and he ventured an opinion. "Nat," he said, "if the instrumentation is bad, how about adding a string section to the trio for this record. It would be completely different and would set a new trend for you."

Nat agreed, but at Capitol Records there was some uncertainty over whether to record it with strings or without. It was eventually tried both ways and the decision was made to go with the strings-added version.

The year was 1947, and "The Christmas Song" has never stopped selling.

A year later, there was "Nature Boy," and still later, the song I thought would never make it. It was a song which Nat had been scheduled to sing in a Paramount movie, but the sequence was deleted and Nat, having been already contracted to do it, was paid. One day soon after Louis Lipsone, who was head of the music department at Paramount, telephoned Carlos and said, "You guys got paid for not working, so will you do me a favor and let Alan Livingston and Ray Evans come over to Nat's house and play him this song."

It was suggested that the pair drop by our house early that evening, but when Nat heard about it, he told Carlos, "I don't want to hear any song at dinner time."

"Well, remember they paid us off on the picture," Carlos argued, "so I guess we have to give and take a little."

"Okay," Nat agreed finally, "let them come by."

Afterwards Nat told Carlos, "Those guys were by here with that Italian song, and I'm going to record it for them, that 'Mona Lisa.' "

"That's not Italian," Carlos told him.

"Well, it sounds Italian," Nat replied.

The song was recorded, and went into a backlog Nat had built up at Capitol.

Then one day in the lobby of the recording firm, as Nat was on his way upstairs on business, a couple of songwriters thrust a song at him and he took it and kept on walking, promising to see them when he came back down.

Meanwhile, Nat looked over the tune and decided, "This is kind of cute. I think it could be a big hit!"

The song was titled "The Greatest Inventor of Them All," and when Nat played and sang it, everybody at Capitol was in agreement that it could be a great hit.

The song was recorded, and as preparations were made to release it, Jim Conkling, then a Capitol vice-president, called Carlos and asked: "What shall we put on the back of 'The Greatest Inventor of Them All?'"

"I don't care," replied Carlos, reflecting almost everyone's attitude that "Greatest Inventor" was going to be such a hit that it really didn't matter about the flip side.

"Well, there's that thing from the movie, called 'Mona Lisa,'" Jim suggested. "If we don't put that out soon, the picture will come out and then the song will be stale."

"Anything will do," Carlos said nonchalantly. The two of them then began discussing something else.

As the song hits began to roll, it became obvious that Nat could not continue to sit at a piano and sing. He was a full-fledged crooner and would have to perform as such. Both Carlos and I encouraged him to do it.

Sometime earlier, Mort Ruby had told Nat that he had dreamt of him performing as a stand-up single. "Gee, I just couldn't," Nat had protested then. "I wouldn't know what to do with my hands."

At the time, Nat still suffered from stage fright. He had gotten a lesson in overcoming it once when, while doing a radio show with disc jockey Al Jarvis, Al tossed a commercial to him and said, "Here, read it. You're on the air."

Nat started to tremble. Jarvis switched the mike off and told him, "Take a deep breath and read it slowly." Nat did as Al flipped the mike on again.

But Nat still could not see himself performing on stage in a solo spot. It happened, however, during a booking in Pittsburgh. Mort had rented three autos for the trio to drive up from Chicago, and everyone was given written instructions as to touring, time, meeting place and all.

Fifteen minutes before time for the show, nobody was there to perform but Nat. The concert promoter was worried, and Mort got on the phone to the State Highway Patrol, checking for a possible accident. There was no word.

Shortly after 8 P.M., customers began chanting and clapping for the show to begin. "Well, I guess we're going to have to cancel the concert," the producer said ruefully.

"No, we're not going to cancel this concert because Nat will do it alone if he has to," Mort declared.

"Well, I've contracted for the King Cole Trio," the promoter declared.

"But even if I can't give you the King Cole Trio, I can give you Nat King Cole," Mort argued. He then went on to propose, "Every ticket price you have to refund, we will make good. I'll go out front and tell the audience."

The curtains were rolled in, the piano moved center-stage and Mort phoned the control booth to hit him with a spotlight when he walked onstage. The audience, still chanting for a show, howled when Mort suddenly appeared in the circle of light. Nat was tall, dark and had a full head of hair. The man they saw was short, Jewish and bald. When the audience quieted, Mort told them, "Due to unforseen circumstances, Nat King Cole is the only member of the trio who has arrived. He is sitting behind the curtain at the piano ready to entertain. If anyone who has bought a ticket feels that you are going to be cheated, you may go to the box office right now and get your money back."

Shouts began to ring out, "We want Nat! We want Nat!"

Mort grinned. "With great pride," he said, "I present to you the one and only Nat King Cole!"

Nat then played for one hour and twenty-five minutes without stopping for anything but applause. Then he took an intermission and played the second half. Two or three times during the performance, he got up and sang a capella, then went back to the piano.

Thus his first performance as a single occurred by accident.

Five minutes before he finished, the remainder of the trio arrived.

But Nat, who became known as a master showman, was a long time getting over his shyness. As he once admitted, "I never looked at the audience, even after years of singing. I was too scared."

7

My marriage to Nat Cole, a wonderful, exciting adventure that was to last seventeen years, was a melding of contrasts, and yet I feel that the very nature of our differences made us a perfect match: Nat had something to give me, and I had something to give him. The only thing we had in common in our backgrounds was religion. He was a Baptist and I an Episcopalian; we were both raised by the Bible. You never lose it. We both believed in prayer, and indeed prayed together many times. When I had attended boarding school, it was Wednesday night prayer meetings and every Sunday church and Sunday school. Nat, of course, as a minister's son, had experienced the same thing, if not more so.

But while Nat's upbringing had been that of a poor Negro boy on the South side of Chicago, the only difference between my childhood and that of a little rich white girl was that I was black. My sisters and I were instructed in—and duly learned—the social graces. We stood when elders entered the room, we ate at the tea table when my aunt had guests. We had nurses to care for us, and never plaited our own pigtails until I was thirteen. Yet, we had our household duties. Aunt Lottie believed in an old-fashioned New England upbringing, but she was a worldly woman. She traveled to Europe long before most black people of means did, and visitors to our home included such people as Mrs. Eleanor Roosevelt, Mrs. Sara Delano Roosevelt (President Franklin D. Roosevelt's mother), W.E.B. DuBois, Langston Hughes, Roland Hayes and Mary McLeod Bethune, most of whom were our house guests from time to time. Aunt Lottie had also authored a book of etiquette entitled *The Correct Thing*.

Perhaps because of the circumstances of our being in her charge, Aunt Lottie put us on a pedestal. My mother had died in Boston during the birth of my sister Carol. I was two then, and seven or eight by the time we were sent by my father, a mail carrier, to live with Aunt Lottie at the Palmer Memorial Institute in Sedalia, North Carolina, during winter months. Despite whatever compassion or favoritism she felt for us, however, Aunt Lottie was quick to see to it that we were punished extra for any temporary infractions, backsliding or general fall from grace, for we were supposed to be examples for the other students at the Institute.

The Institute itself was founded by my aunt in 1902 and supported by very wealthy New England families, principally the Galen Stones, Alice Freeman Palmer (after whom the institute was named) and Charles Elliott.

The people who lived around the Institute in those days were what was referred to as "poor white trash," but they loved my aunt and respected her. It was usually "Yes, ma'am, Dr. Brown," a rare mark of respect paid to a black person by Southern whites in those times.

When we went to buy clothes in nearby Greensboro, the saleswomen would slip my sister and me into the dressing rooms because of my aunt. Stores, as a rule, didn't permit black people to try on clothes then.

About the only real prejudice we faced was when a bunch of us from the school would board a bus and go into town to the Carolina Theater, where we had to sit in the balcony with the downstairs section reserved for whites. After a while my aunt just stopped us from going. But I remember some of the fine stage productions we saw: *Green Pastures*, *The Merchant of Venice* and *Hansel and Gretel*.

We lived with my aunt in a house called Canary Cottage —she always had a canary, and I hated them. It was a beautiful white, New England-style, two-story house with a huge living room, four upstairs bedrooms and two baths, which was a luxury in those days, as was the telephone. There were lovely grounds surrounding the cottage.

My sister and I (sometimes both sisters were there, but the youngest, Babe, did not always stay with us, living most of the time with my family back in Massachusetts) paid little attention to the famous visitors who came, taking them for granted and most times being shunted out of the way while the adults made intellectual conversation. In my aunt's house we children were mainly concerned with studying and church and teas and Wednesday night prayers. We arose at seven each weekday morning to prepare for school and we were not permitted to dawdle, either mornings or evenings, listening to the radio, which brought us the outside world. I used to die waiting for Friday nights and a program featuring singer Frances Langford.

Movie magazines were the "in" reading in those days, and when I went home in the summers I lived by them. It only cost eight cents to go to the movies, and that was my life, sweetened more so by the usual accompanying bag of jelly doughnuts.

Back at the Institute there were occasional dances, strictly chaperoned, and you didn't dare dance too close to a boy, either. I remember once, when I was about fifteen, my aunt telling one young man sternly, "If she ever lies down, you had better walk over her."

My aunt traveled a lot, and I confess that my sister and I were happy to see her go. But when she would return we would be just as happy to see her, and once in a while she would bring us something nice.

We had marvelous Christmases, too, because my aunt made a big thing out of them. We always had a beautiful tree and lovely outfits that she would bring us from up North. There was a big warm fireplace and lots of gifts and succulent roast beef for the holiday. (Perhaps because of this, throughout the years that Nat and I were married, and even today, I put a lot of effort into Christmas cele-brations.)

My aunt was not a wealthy woman, but like other black professionals of that era in the South who were not welcome at country clubs, fine hotels and restaurants or other places where money might be easily spent, she managed to live comfortably within the confines of her home. She was a no-nonsense-type person whose unusual intelligence had been spotted early by people who were able to help with her education, and her approach to financial matters mirrored these qualities. In addition to her salary at the Institute, she was in considerable demand as a guest speaker, which caused her to travel often, as did her continuing efforts to raise money for the school.

There were trips where Charlotte and I went along, and when we traveled anywhere, we went in our own car, or if it was a long distance, we traveled by train in Pullmans. I vaguely remember the curtain sometimes being pulled to segregate us when we went into dining cars, but only a couple of times, because we almost always carried a lunch basket or just did not go to the diner because we were too proud to be insulted.

Christmas and travel were the rare fun times, however, when we were in my aunt's charge. She ruled supreme over our lives, demanding discipline, rigorous schoolwork, love of God, and attention to our manners.

So while young Nathaniel Adams Coles was reared on religion and jazz, the early years of Maria Hawkins were comprised of religion and finishing school. Needless to say, Nat's world, when I entered it in the late forties, was the more fascinating. There were the lights, the crowds, the applause, the press interviews, the train and bus rides from Chicago to Omaha to Minneapolis to Springfield to Detroit; to Kansas City, Witchita and Denver; Salt Lake City, San Francisco and Los Angeles. Long theater dates in New York and Cleveland, and one night stands in Birmingham, Tuskegee, Macon, Raleigh, Charleston and Atlanta.

Becoming Mrs. Nat Cole, of course, had meant the end of Maria Ellington's career as a singer. He made it perfectly clear that he was quite able to support a wife, and, for all of my own thoughts about becoming a star, I have to admit that I was quite happy in my new role. (There came a time during our marriage when, just because I was a little annoyed with my husband, I decided to take another fling at a career of my own. I put together my own act, and on opening night at Ciro's I got a standing ovation and good reviews.

Afterward, I did a couple of Ed Sullivan appearances with Nat. It was not long, however, before Nat decided he had been right the first time: he would be the singer; I would be his wife, and that was that. I had enjoyed the stage while I held it, but it was nice to have my man order me home again.)

When we were first married, we discussed having a baby. Nat wanted one immediately, but I certainly didn't. All I could think of was that having a child meant I wouldn't be with him all the time.

When we did one-nighters, we traveled by Pullman.

Sometimes we did thirty such shows in a stretch. On occasion, I would get ill with all the riding, but I wouldn't tell Nat. I was so much in love with him and so determined to stay with him.

There were happy times and funny times. Like watching Nat get up in the mornings. He wore mini-length night-shirts and house-shoes so old they would fall apart before he would give them up. For a full five minutes he would walk around as if still asleep, not saying anything to anybody. I would look at him and those feet in those big floppy shoes and kid, "Honey, if I had seen your feet first, I never would have married you." (Those same feet were bad enough to have kept Nat out of military service during World War II. Nat told me later he was so happy to learn he wasn't being drafted that he jumped into his pants and shirt and ran out of the medical examination building without his underwear.)

There were always newspaper reporters and fans wanting to know what our life was like, and I tried to tell them some of the routine. Living out of a suitcase on the road was no bed of roses for anyone, I explained, and it certainly wasn't for us. But Nat was a real trouper who took it all in stride, and nothing really bothered him except perhaps my cloud of wet stockings strung up on shower doors in so many hotel rooms. He liked to eat everything, which was just as well. As I explained it to one reporter, "Contrary to public opinion, I am no cook. About the only thing I can make well is gingerbread."

For all my upbringing, the one thing I was not taught to do was cook, simply because I did not like it. One of my last culinary disasters came while we were staying in an apartment at the Watkins Hotel in Los Angeles before we bought a home. My friend Mildred Bruce (who is now married to Sugar Ray Robinson) came up and showed me how to prepare a few things, so one night I invited her to dinner with Nat and me to show off my skills. To a menu of lamb chops and mashed potatoes, I added strawberry shortcake, an item Millie had not included in her crash course in cookery. As I sat the dessert before the diners, one side went one way and one went another, as the whole cake collapsed. I cried, Millie went into hysterics and Nat couldn't stop laughing.

But sitting around that apartment all day while Nat was out taking care of business gave me time to learn to cook one thing well: old-style, homemade gingerbread. To this day, it is the best thing I make and Nat loved it. As for the rest of my cooking, Nat could do without it.

But there were other things in marriage that Nat chose not to do without. One of them was children.

We were on a string of one-nighters when, in North Carolina, I told Nat's valet, Sparky, I wasn't feeling well. Sparky was more than just an employee; he was one of the family, and as such, he became the first to know.

"What's the matter with you?" he demanded in that gruff voice of his when I told him I felt ill.

"I think—I'm not sure—but I think I'm pregnant."

"Well, don't say nothin' if you're not sure," Sparky warned. We both knew how much Nat wanted a child, and we did not want to raise any false hopes.

The group was heading for Mississippi about that time, and Nat felt it might be too rough trying to find suitable accommodations for us, so he sent me home from the tour temporarily. I went immediately to see our family doctor, who confirmed my suspicions. I telephoned Nat long distance and told him in a sing-song voice, "You're going to be a papa!" He was delirious with joy.

Before the happiness of our first child, however, there would be tragedy. My youngest sister, Carol, whom we called Babe, had not been feeling well in New York, and I had taken her to see a doctor, who failed to find any real illness. Later she went home to Boston, and while Nat was on a date there, we took Babe out to dinner. She looked thin and pale to us then, and she was coughing. The next thing I knew, she was in a hospital. I went to see her. She looked so slim and small, wasted away in less than two and one half months. On Mother's Day, we brought her three-and-a-half-year-old daughter, nicknamed Cookie, out to the hospital courtyard so that she could wave up to her mother in the window. It was a sad time.

A new drug had just come onto the market then, streptomycin, but the young doctor attending Babe told us it was just like giving her water. The treatment of the tuberculosis had begun too late. In just a few short days, Babe was dead.

My grandmother had died when I was fifteen, my mother when I was two, and now, losing the same sister that my mother had died giving birth to was a tremendous shock to me. We were extremely close. I think I took it worse than I might have because we had all been unaware of anything wrong with her for so long. If we had known in time, it wouldn't have had to happen. She was twenty-two years old.

Looking back, it seems that death has always been hovering in the wings: my mother, Babe, even my first husband, Spurgeon Neal Ellington, an Army Air Force Lieutenant, whom I had married in 1943. He flew combat missions in Italy with the 332nd Fighter Group and was awarded the Distinguished Flying Cross. Considered an excellent pilot and back in the States only a short while, he had just visited me in New York when, on December 10, 1945, during a routine training flight back to his base at Tuskegee, Alabama, he crashed.

In May of 1949, however, my thoughts were on Cookie, for Babe's death left her an orphan, as her father had also died the previous year. I telephoned Nat from the hospital to give him the news of Babe's death.

"Where's Cookie?" he asked almost immediately.

"She's here. One of us in the family will have to—"

I didn't get to finish.

"We'll take her!" Nat said quickly.

"Are you sure?" I asked him.

"Of course!" he almost shouted, he was so excited.

My sister Charlotte legally would have had the first right to Cookie, being the eldest. But I was married and well off, and Charlotte, at the time, was still single, and was therefore willing to give her over to me. "You should keep her," Charlotte told me, and the grandparents on both sides agreed.

We were all in agreement, it turned out, except Aunt Lottie, who maintained her position as matriarch of the family. Even though she was in her sixties, she wanted Cookie, and being accustomed to making decisions and running things, she was determined to have her. Not quite realizing it herself, I suppose, she was at a stage of life where, having lost all of us to adulthood, she wanted another child to rear.

We finally had to go into court to settle it, unfortunate as it was. But Nat had been just as stubborn on this matter as had been Aunt Lottie. "You might run your family," he told her, "but you don't run mine."

Aunt Lottie did not win of course, and it was very sad for her to lose something so late in life. But she had clashed with Nat on one of the few occasions in his life when he was not willing to yield. By nature a very soft and gentle man, Nat could, at extremely rare intervals, stand up and roar. And when he did, we all sat very quietly.

Cookie went on the road with us for seven and a half months, then I came home to have my first baby, Natalie, whom we soon started to call "Sweetie." I would not have come home then had not Nat made me do so. I cried and cried on the plane home so that I became nauseated and vomited.

When Sweetie was five weeks old, I headed right back out on the road. I could not hold back my desire to be with him, and I asked my doctor about it. "Is there something wrong with me?" I asked. "I love my baby but I'd rather be with my husband."

"Maria," he told me, "go back with your husband. That's where you belong because when this child is sixteen, it isn't going to make any difference to her at all whether you were there or not when she was five weeks old."

So I left Sweetie and Cookie at home with a nurse, and I never had a guilty conscience about it. However, we never missed an important time in their lives, such as birthdays, holidays and graduations.

From those early days until the very last, whenever I was going out to meet Nat, it was very exciting, like a fairy tale. At first, when we were on the road and found ourselves in a room with twin beds, we would sleep together in one. (But five years later I tried that and couldn't sleep.) I was so much in love with Nat that when he went out to work, I'd get one of his jackets from the closet and put it around me just to smell it.

During much of our early travel in the South, we were obliged to stay in other people's homes, since hotel accommodations for Negroes frequently ranged from poor to nonexistent. (I could swear, for instance, that I became pregnant with Sweetie during a one-night performance in Montgomery, Alabama, Nat's home town, where he drew probably 276 people—all of them relatives.)

Some places, of course, had homes that became known for housing black entertainers, because of them all being forced to seek quarters across the tracks, so to speak. One that I remember best of all was a boarding house in Washington, D.C., operated by a woman named Edwina. Performers came to eat or sleep, with their wives or a companion, at Edwina's—she never asked any questions.

Edwina served liquor in her kitchen, and seemingly knew personally all the policemen in town. I can still remember her calling good-bye to us after a stay there; and, then to

Sparky, whose name she never seemed to remember, she would say, "Good-bye, young man."

It was at Edwina's that I first tried the soul-food delicacy chitlins, and pretty soon I could out-eat Nat. Once in Little Rock, Arkansas, I even ordered them for breakfast. "I have never," commented Nat, laughing, "seen anything so ridiculous in my life."

I loved every minute of it, because I loved everything about Nat Cole—even the things I must admit I gradually helped to change. As every woman knows, no man is perfect. It is only through patience, determination and an eye for detail that a woman is able to create something near perfection in a husband. Naturally, all of this is tempered by love.

Nat had one overwhelming weakness, and he never succeeded in overcoming it: he was as gullible a man as ever lived. I used to say my husband was the kind of person who, had be been a woman, would have been pregnant all the time, because he couldn't say No to anybody. He was a man who could find some good in everybody. This, coupled with the fact that he was naturally generous to a fault, presented his new bride with quite a challenge. I remembered getting out of a cab one night when we were courting and, in utter amazement, watched Nat peel off nearly a thousand dollars in large bills as he tried to find some smaller ones with which to pay the fare. That's when I decided quietly to myself: when we get married, I handle the money.

Nat had no established credit, paid cash for everything, and always carried large sums of loose bills—never neatly— in his pockets. I had never heard of such a thing.

Clothing styles, naturally, change as a matter of course

over the years, but with Nat it was more than just a style change; his own taste changed from some of the more garish combinations that were musician-fads, and I am flattered to think that I was instrumental in tailoring his preference to a more conservative tone. In time he became known for his sartorial elegance.

As for money, Nat placed absolutely no value in it. He worked for the sheer joy of working, and we would probably have always been broke if I had not liked all the comforts of life that result from making money. But I think during that period so many people in show business thought very little about their financial future. Perhaps it's because they didn't really want to consider the day when they might retire from all the acclaim. But I used to tell Nat, "I have no intention of being poor when we are old. I don't want to look at anybody in our September years and envy them because they're living like I used to."

I had thought that way before I married Nat, and I believe in time I brought him around to thinking that way too. I knew my husband would make money as long as he wanted to work, but there was a time when I was foolish enough to think that he might want to retire at a certain age. Later, however, I realized he never would have retired.

But in the early days of our marriage, this was a long time away, although Nat's weakness was already in evidence. I can remember once Nat sent an employee off to Western Union with $750 to be wired to someone. In due time, it was learned that the money never reached its destination. A little checking soon showed the reason why: the cash never even reached Western Union. Nevertheless, the person responsible for wiring the money insisted he had sent it, and despite the fact that no receipt for the money was ever produced, or that the money was never seen again, there was no doubt in Nat's mind that the man was telling the truth—Western Union simply had to be in error.

I suppose one of the earliest crises in Nat's career came when Oscar Moore and Johnny Miller, his original accompanists, decided to quit. I had told Nat that the salaries he was paying were ridiculously high, and that inasmuch as it was his voice and name that was drawing the money in, he should take the lion's share. Oscar and Johnny objected to this point of view, of course, and they quit. Nat worried greatly about it at first, but I soon convinced him that the Nat King Cole style rested primarily with him rather than those around him.

I was rough and I will admit it. But I know my real concern was for my husband, and I did not care what others thought. I did what I felt I had to do to protect him, and although it wasn't easy, most of those who resented me in those first years later became my good friends. But Nat was never a natural-born leader, and I had to make him one at the risk of no one liking me. Even Carlos Gastel and I fought for years after I married Nat. When we fell in love with and bought a beautiful home, Carlos was among those who criticized our seeming extravagance. (What everyone really seemed to have been saying was that it was too nice a place for Negroes.) "Why not?" I demanded when I faced Carlos. "You bought one, didn't you?"

"Yes," he replied, "but mine doesn't look like this."

"Why should it?" I shot back. "You're his manager. If it did look like this, I'd begin to wonder what you were doing with his money."

Nat's environment became entirely different after we

married, and he began to meet the type of people I thought he should. I admit I was ambitious, but only for him; for, above all, I loved him.

Truthfully, there were times when I did not enjoy the role I had to play, when I wished my husband were a stronger man, for there were signs of great weakness in him that no woman likes. But no human is perfect, and I am sure that there were times when Nat wished I didn't seem to know so much.

People thought of me as being tough and strong, but what they probably didn't realize was that I had to be; I had no choice. What they don't know is that when Nat put his foot down, that was it. The fact is that I could never have had the influence upon Nat's life had he not permitted me to do so. He *wanted* me to do the things I did, to give advice and take action in those areas where he felt my judgment was best.

I basically am not quite as extroverted as I always had to be, but I've always been independent. I've always known what I wanted out of life. I think this accounts for my aggressiveness and my strength. Yet basically I don't think I ever really wanted to use those qualities in a marriage.

I have a great desire to be needed. I believe in astrology, and my sign is Leo. I am very honest and sincere, but I must be needed. Leos have tremendous drive and sense of leadership, and Pisces, under which my husband was born, is not suposed to be a good sign opposite mine, but he had his own drive in a completely different direction: his music.

He was more tolerant than I, and I am much more tolerant today because of him. Nat's temperament was calm, like the sea: Pisces, the fish. I am just the opposite: Leo, the lion. I would rant and rave, but then I was through with it, for I am not a sulker. Nor am I a dreamer, but a tremendous romanticist.

The great attraction that Nat held for me was that he was a very gentle man. To me, a man should be firm, but gentle. In Nat's case he happened to need my strength. He had the talent, but there were other things he didn't have to go with it as far as business was concerned. Nat Cole was an introspective man, and sometimes a little afraid of himself. I think that the same reason he was unable to express egotism about his success was the reason why he was so great on the stage. I don't think he ever really believed it could all happen to him. He was the most "un-celebrity-like" person on earth, extremely grateful for what had happened to him.

Ours was a true love affair. There were little things like kissing every night, and there were times when I sat in his lap. We preferred to share our time together at home, rather than spend much of it in separate parts of the house. I remember waking Nat up from snoring one night and chiding him with: "Gosh, honey, we're going to have to get twin beds."

"There'll be no twin beds in here!" he told me quickly.

I loved it when he said that.

As I mentioned before, from the very beginning, I went on the road with my husband. Other wives of entertainers criticized me for it at the time, but I have lived to see the day when many of them now follow their husbands on the road.

I have never for one moment regretted the years I spent traveling with my husband, for I know that I was there to help him when he needed me, to guide him when he faltered, to praise him when he succeeded, and to share in our maturing together. In a way, Nat was one of the most remarkable men I have ever seen in my life, for he was one of the few people I have known who actually acquired class. He did it all: a certain stature, a certain amount of poise, and the only reason I can think of for his having acquired it is because he wanted to. In the years that followed, I was made proud by the fact that people who knew me could see a certain amount of Maria Cole in the Nat Cole who appeared on stage.

8

The plane out of Philadelphia that March morning in 1951 was bound for Los Angeles, but for the Nat Cole party aboard, it was: destination—trouble.

I tried to nap during the trip, to blot everything out, but sleep was always impossible for us on planes. Nat was beside me, reading a book or pretending to, but I knew what was going on in his mind. There could be but one thing: our home in Los Angeles, and how we were going to lose it.

The story was in all the newspapers: "COLE HOME SEIZED BY GOVERNMENT." According to the Bureau of Internal Revenue, as it was then known, we owed the Government $146,000 in unpaid taxes. Nat, who was earning about $200,000 a year at the time, had in the last twelve months paid some $66,000 in current and back taxes, and now was offering another $50,000 on the account. But the Government refused it, took away our 1949 Cadillac, and ordered that the house be sold to satisfy its claim. We had one week in which to get out.

With Nat, the house had been a matter of love at first sight, and we had already gone through a tremendous ordeal for it.

When we first married, I had suggested that we live in New England or Connecticut. After all, Nat had been married and lived in Los Angeles before, so I thought I was giving him an out by suggesting the East Coast.

"Are you kidding?" he asked me. "I love Los Angeles, and we're going right out there to live."

For six months we had lived in an apartment hotel, and then we found our house. We had no more than walked into the front hallway when Nat rubbed his chin with his fingertips and declared, "This is it!"

I was astonished. "What do you mean, 'this is it'?" I asked him. "I haven't seen the bathrooms or the closets or the kitchen or . . ."

"This is it," he repeated.

And it was. For all my husband's gentleness, when his mind was made up, he was like the Rock of Gibraltar.

The house was magnificent, a twelve-room English Tudor-style home with a three-car garage and servants' quarters up over it. The living room was huge, 33 by 16 feet with a twelve-foot-high ceiling. The master bedroom upstairs was the same size. It was, of course, quite expensive by 1948 standards: $85,000. But everyone could see that even at that price it was a good buy. And Nat had said this was it. Now the problems began.

The house of our choice was located in the heart of Los Angeles' oldest and wealthiest neighborhood, Hancock Park, where the governor of the state, doctors, lawyers and some of California's most genteel, "nicest" people lived, all in the warmth and protection of a fifty-year restrictive covenant barring the area to anybody whose skin was not white. It was an area where holy hell was about to break loose.

A Negro real estate man had shown us the house, which was being handled by a white realtor acquaintance of his. The home had been built and owned originally by William Lacey, a former president of the Los Angeles City Chamber of Commerce. It was later sold to its then present owners. The new purchaser of this house, it was understood, would have to be white.

Our agent produced a "white" woman purchaser—a Negro woman of such light skin that there was no reason to question her racial origin. She walked into the real estate office one morning and laid six $1,000 bills on the desk and the deal began to move. In the end, a $35,000 down payment was made on the home, and the "white" buyer transferred the property to Mr. and Mrs. Nat Cole.

That's when the spit hit the fan.

The Los Angeles Times began a story the next morning, "Residents of Hancock Park, one of the city's most exclusive residential districts, admittedly were in a quandary yesterday concerning the purchase of one of the neighborhood's finest homes by Nat King Cole, Negro singer and entertainer."

In a "quandary" indeed! The neighborhood was about to have a collective stroke!

A couple of nights later I got a call at the hotel from an attorney friend. "I just drove by the house you bought," he said, "and I don't know what's going on but people are walking back and forth in front of the place and the police are there."

Nat was working that evening, so I went over myself. When I arrived I asked a police officer what was happening.

"I don't know, lady," he said, "you'll have to. . . ." And his voice kind of trailed off and was lost in the noise. People were strolling by, muttering to each other as if the house were a body at a wake. "I remember when the Laceys first moved in here," I heard one old man remark sadly to his wife.

Hancock Park residents, however, did more than just march and mutter. They formed a protest group and picked Andrew J. Copp, Jr., an attorney, as their chairman. Copp showed up one night at Ciro's on the Sunset Strip where Nat was appearing. "I want to talk to Nat Cole," he told Mort Ruby.

"Can you give me an idea of what you want to talk to him about?" Mort asked.

"Yes. Tell Mr. Cole that if he will rescind the sale of his house, we will give him his money back with a little profit."

Mort went to Nat and they discussed the situation. "What do you think I ought to tell him?" Nat asked.

"Why don't you tell him that if they'll give you a million dollars, you'll leave the country," Mort suggested.

"All right"—Nat grinned—"go on out and tell him."

There was no reason for the people of Hancock Park to object to our moving in, of course, except the color of our skin. We were certainly people who could afford the house, and we were people of good background, comparable, I would dare say, to any of the other residents and probably surpassing that of some. Almost all of the residents were older people, and I was quite young at the time. But I knew that there would have been no objection if, say, a Rockefeller daughter moved in. Well, I was married and my husband wanted to buy me the house as a honeymoon gift. Nat explained it to the public as honestly as he could.

"This is not an act of defiance," he announced. "My bride and I like this house. I can afford it, and we would like to make it our home. I have always been a good citizen. I would like to meet all my new neighbors face to face and explain these things to them."

Later, Nat got his chance to talk with some of the residents at a meeting of the neighborhood association, where it was patiently explained to my husband that the good people of Hancock Park simply did not want any undesirables moving in.

"Neither do I," said Nat. "And if I see anybody undesirable coming in here, I'll be the first to complain."

Nat would have his house. The U.S. Supreme Court had just ruled that restrictive covenants were null and void, and on August 13, 1948, my husband and I moved into Hancock Park.

Now, on this March day in 1951, we were flying home to new trouble there, trouble which, I honestly feel to this day, stemmed from the fact we had never been wanted in the neighborhood. Not only had people been angry with us, but the office of the real estate agent had been deluged with complaints about her negotiating the sale. "Don't you check out the people you sell to?" she was often asked.

"I sure do," she would shoot back. "As soon as they walk in the door, I ask them, 'Have you got the down payment?' "

Eventually her life was threatened, and a police patrol was assigned to look out for her.

Yes, the law seemed to have been on our side then, but now it was the U.S. Government demanding a huge sum of money, a sum we simply could not pay all at once. "I owe the money, all right," Nat admitted. "I'm not trying to cheat the Government, but I want time to pay."

The debt had come about as it often does to people who suddenly find themselves making large sums of money: a basic lack of understanding of tax laws, poor record-keeping, and in some cases, mismanagement.

But the Government was not interested in why, or in granting time. It was interested only in $146,000. We were flying home to face that demand.

"Mr. Cole," someone said suddenly on the plane, "may I have your autograph?"

Across the aisle from us, a man stirred in the seat next to Sparky, Nat's valet. "Pardon me," he said to Sparky, "but is that Nat King Cole?"

"Yeah," Sparky grunted.

"I'd like to talk to him."

"Well, I don't think this would be the time, right now," Sparky told him. "He's going home and he's not in the mood for talking."

The man persisted, however, and introduced himself to us as Phil Braunstein, an accountant with offices in New York and Los Angeles. He, like everyone else, had read about our tax problems. He and his partner on the West Coast, Harold Plant, seemed to specialize in the business affairs of entertainment people.

"Maybe you can help us," I suggested to him.

Phil gave us his card as we left the plane in Los Angeles, and suggested we telephone him.

Nat and I then drove out to the house—the house plastered with the signs announcing Government seizure—and faced my sister, Charlotte, and my friend Hannah

Daniels, who had borne the brunt of the whole thing. "They've been very nasty about it all," Charlotte explained, irked by the rude invasion of tax agents. Not only had they posted their signs and driven off our car, they had also searched for anything else of value. "They even started for the piano," Charlotte declared, "and I told them. 'Don't you dare touch that piano!'" Then, with an impish grin, she continued. "By the way, Sis, 'my' furs are still intact, in case you want to 'borrow' them!"

She and Hannah had already stored "their silverware."

It was an ugly time, as if the world was coming to an end overnight. Nat lay in bed that night, smoking one cigarette after another. I tried to reassure him, "We can start all over if we have to, I really don't care."

But Nat, who under normal circumstances could fall asleep instantly, for the only time in the seventeen years we were married lay awake far into the night.

9

The tragedy we now faced was by no means new to celebrities. Nat Cole, like many a performer or fighter or businessman before him, suddenly found himself making more money than he had ever dreamed of. And there were so many things to do, so many things to buy.

I was mystified by it all, for the greater part of the indebtedness had been incurred in the years before our marriage. And Nat, typically, found no one to blame but himself. In later years, Carlos Gastel was to remark, "He could have blamed me, he could have blamed his accountant, but he didn't. When it happened, all he said was, 'It was my own fault.'"

Whose fault it was mattered little now. The problem was not only one of the amount owed to the Federal Government, but it was a situation that could pyramid for a man in Nat's financial bracket. If he used the money he was then making to pay off the back taxes, he would still be incurring heavy new taxes on the current income—new taxes that would also have to be paid. It was an ever-spiraling, ever more entangling, ever-worsening situation.

To make matters even more galling, some of the questioning my husband was subjected to was downright insulting. A Southern-oriented investigator, for instance, wanted to know why Nat lived in such a fine house, and why he had to carry so much life insurance. His implication was clear: for black people, we were, in his opinion, living too high off the hog.

Indeed, the future could hardly have looked bleaker, and the only ray of sun shining through, although we could barely have recognized it as such at the time, was the chance plane meeting with Phil Braunstein.

When Phil arrived at his Los Angeles office, he told his West Coast partner, Harold Plant, about his conversation with us on the plane. "It looks like a pretty rough thing," Harold told Phil. "Nat needs a great deal of help."

Fortunately for us, they were able to provide it. Phil and Harold Plant became much more than just business advisers; they became our friends. The first time Nat went to their offices to discuss the tax problem, the men talked for a long while, then broke for lunch. As they walked down the hall, still talking, Nat slipped his arm around Harold's shoulder, a small, innocent but warm gesture that Harold never forgot. As he explained many years later, "It made me feel very odd and very proud, because I suddenly came to realize that Nat had not only accepted me as an accountant and business manager, but as a friend. It meant a great deal to me." Even since my husband's death, this friendship remains.

With the intervention of Harold and Phil as our business representatives, the Internal Revenue Service became a little more agreeable, at least to the extent of accepting an arrangement whereby we could begin to pay our tax debt without loss of our home or other possessions. Robert Riddell, then head of the Southern California District of the Internal Revenue Service, agreed to an arrangement with Phil and Harold whereby a cash payment of $50,000 was to be made to the Government immediately, and other minimum payments to be made periodically on the balance owed. There was a further stipulation that Nat, who began working an engagement at the Tiffany Club in Los Angeles while the negotiations were going on, would make payments of $1,000 weekly on his current taxes.

To raise the initial $50,000 cash, we went to my aunt, and suddenly her need to be needed was fulfilled. Gone was her resentment of my having married Nat in the first place; gone, too, was her bitterness over our having fought it out in the courts over custody of Cookie. All Aunt Lottie thought about now was that we needed her, and she could help. It was one of the last occasions in her lifetime of giving of herself that she would be asked to give again.

Her reply to our call for help came by Western Union —$20,000.

The remaining $30,000 was advanced by Capitol Records under a new contract which would provide additional advances over the next three years, all to go to the Government. Capitol's guarantee was for a total of $120,000 over a four-year period, with any royalty money accruing at Capitol to be held in a deferred payment account. Nat had already enjoyed a couple of years during which he earned much more than the new Capitol advance guarantees would seem to indicate, but he was still a relatively new artist on the scene.

He did not stay new for long, for now it seemed as if it had been willed that Nat King Cole would know nothing but one professional success after another. He slapped his hit records back to back.

The quality of sound my husband voiced in song tested the imagination of many. They called his voice silky, or velvety or syrupy or hoarse or honeyed. One writer thought it was "pussy-willow soft." It was Nat's own contention that these descriptions were all generous to excess. "I can't sing," he often said, and he was fond of remembering: "A doctor heard me one night and told me, 'Son, with that throat, you ought to be home in bed.' "

There were those who were inclined to agree with Nat and the doctor, but only to a point, for they heard, and isolated, the deeper qualities of the Cole talent.

As late as 1964, Gene Grove was to write in the *New York Post:* "The voice issues still, as it has for twenty-five years, from a wide, wide mouth to caress a wide, wide world with rock-candy clarity, a two-octave range, and the husky timbre of a hum through a paper-covered comb. It is lovely, but it is still not a lot of voice. . . . Nat Cole and Ethel Merman are two of the toughest singers for a poor lyricist; Miss Merman with her sheer volume and Cole with his precise enunciation will make certain everyone in the house hears every lousy word."

But now, in the spring of 1951, we were involved in a fight for our lives. A contingent part of the settlement agreement, as set out by the tax men, was that there be a quarterly accounting to the Internal Revenue Service, so that the Government could be constantly aware of how much income we had and how much we were spending for both business and personal needs. Harold Plant and

Phil Braunstein were asked to handle all of our financial affairs, including supervision and preparation of the quarterly report.

Despite my husband's comfortable income, the next few years were not easy ones. With so much money going to back taxes, current taxes and expenses, the amount we had left to live on, while certainly adequate, by no means allowed us the sort of limitless luxuries that someone, by simply reading how much Nat earned each week, might suspect. Nat never worked for money but nevertheless enjoyed spending it, as did I. And I have to feel, without any immodesty whatsoever, that it was my knowledge of what a dollar meant and the thrift motto of "spend half and save half" that guided us through this period.

At the end of four years, we had made a substantial dent in the money owed. Nat's career continued to climb swiftly and the $30,000 that Capitol paid each year (and which went immediately to the Government) became only a small portion of the royalties earned. Soon, we found ourselves with more than $100,000 in accrued royalties at Capitol. Still, by contract, this money was not payable to my husband.

Nevertheless, at the end of September, 1954, the Hollywood Tax Office called Harold Plant in and the man in charge pointed out that despite the steady payments of a complicated back-taxes and current-taxes situation, the amount still owed came to $91,000. "Look, I want that Capitol money," he said. "You've got it sitting there, so let's get all these back taxes paid off."

Harold told him that by contract, Nat could not collect the money. "If you insist that we take it," Harold told him, "and even if Capitol is willing to give it to us, that will put us in a severe tax problem again for this year because it will constitute income."

I cannot say that the tax people were so obtuse as not to see our problem; on the other hand, they were not overcome with sympathy. With the myopia that seems to afflict the collectors of the Government's due, all they could see was that they had an unclosed case on the books, and that there was money there somewhere and they wanted it.

And so a new arrangement had to be worked out with us, Capitol and the tax people in which we went to Bank of America and borrowed $90,000, which we were to pay back over a four-year period from deferred royalty payments from Capitol. At the same time, we renegotiated a new contract with Capitol Records because it was now quite apparent that Nat's records were earning more than $30,000 yearly on a consistent basis, and that someday we would have a rather large sum of money we would have to take, thus creating another monster in the form of a brand-new tax problem. The new contract guaranteed Nat $50,000 a year, while the bank was paid off at the rate of $22,500 a year. Even so, with the grace of Nat's God-given talents, the deferred royalty account eventually reached over a million dollars.

When the final payments to the Government were made, a tax official admitted to Harold Plant, "I never thought they would be able to pay this off. I thought we were just letting them stay in that house for a couple of years longer, but I never thought they could pull themselves out of that terrible hole they were in."

I could have told him: neither did we.

10

There were sides of my husband, of course, that only a few people ever saw: the insecure Nat, the humorous Nat, the argumentative Nat. His stage performances were so polished, his musicianship so stylish, his lyrics so silken, his manners so impeccable and easygoing that his millions of admirers might find it difficult to picture a man who never, during his entire lifetime, quite accepted the fact that he was as famous as he was; a man who bit his nails and sometimes anguished over small decisions, a man who often held deep convictions beneath an outer layer of soft pliability, a man who loved private debate, who, while never vulgar yet had a complete command of profanity, and who, in almost everything, had a wonderful sense of humor.

Sometimes the humor wasn't exactly intentional, such as back in 1945, when Nat took his first plane ride. The aircraft was a DC-3, provided by the Army to transport him to a military base to do a benefit performance for GI's. The plane taxied to the end of the runway and began to rev up its engines. The engines raced and raced, louder and louder, with the plane cabin seemingly straining under the roar until Nat finally turned to Mort Ruby in the next seat and asked, "How high do you think we are now?"

"Nat," Mort answered patiently, "we haven't left the ground yet."

There were times when Nat's humor was deliberate and carried a touch of irony, such as when he pulled a practical joke on his agency, General Artists Corporation. During his early days with them, Nat had bought a used car, and while playing Nick's in the Village, had found himself unable to meet a month's note, $17.50. Nat went to GAC for an advance and was refused. Years later, while earning $5,000 a week at the Paramount in New York, Nat told Mort Ruby about the incident, and the two decided to test the agency's current attitude toward a now star performer. "Go over and see what you can get," Nat told Mort.

Mort went over and faced the same GAC executive who had refused the $17.50 loan. "Nat wants to borrow twenty-five hundred dollars," Mort told him solemnly.

The GAC official snapped his fingers, called in his secretary and ordered a check drawn up immediately.

Mort accepted it and took it to Nat at his Paramount dressing room. Nat looked at it for a few moments and then gave Mort a somewhat rueful smile. "Take it back and tell him I don't need it," he said.

Thank goodness my husband enjoyed a good laugh, for there were times when the joke was on him. Ironically, the biggest of all, perhaps, was perpetrated by Mr. Pep, our boxer dog who really became a member of the family and whose own fourteen-year life span ended only weeks before that of his master. When Nat played Los Angeles engagements, Mr. Pep was always there to meet him when he came home at night, and the two of them would make a predawn raid on the kitchen refrigerator, then they would come upstairs to the bedroom together.

But once, just before leaving on a trip, Nat went out and bought a birthday cake as a surprise for me. He hid it in the maid's quarters where Cookie, who was about seven at the time, went in to take a look at it and inadvertently left the door ajar when she came out. Later, while Nat and I were packing, Mr. Pep came up the stairs with white goo on his face. "What is this all over your mouth?" I fussed gently, trying to clean it off. Soon he disappeared, only to show up a few minutes later, wagging his tail and his mouth all white again.

When we went downstairs to dinner a little later, I heard the nurse say to Nat, "Mr. Cole, did Cookie tell you what I told her to tell you?"

"What?" Nat asked.

"Just go on in the back room," she said, and kept on with her work.

Nat went in, and suddenly let out a yell: "Goddamn, you son of a bitch!" He slammed the door, grabbed a paper and for a while it sounded like two men inside fighting. Nat was swinging and Mr. Pep was ducking. When they came out, Mr. Pep's mouth was still white and the surprise birthday cake had been eaten clean to the center.

Nat forgave Mr. Pep just as he forgave friends who did him wrong. He was loyal to them all and in many cases loaned people money which he must have forgotten about the minute he gave it to them. If he got to know you and had faith in you, that was it. You were in.

Among his friends, there was nothing Nat liked more than a good debate, especially about politics, and sports, the latter of which he was extremely knowledgeable. With a couple of drinks to stimulate him, he could engage in good-natured argument half the night. He did it with Carlos and Oscar on trains, with Sparky in hotel rooms and night-club dressing rooms, with friends around the bar at home.

Yet Nat did not like angry argument. Ofttimes, when I would jump on him about something, he would let it pass until I was out of the room and then laugh and ask Sparky, "What did I do now?"

Nat preferred not to speak unkindly even about people he didn't admire. Generally when the conversation drifted around to someone he didn't particularly like, Nat would scratch his chin and remark: "Oh, he's all right." And, if he had respect for you and felt that you were doing something for an adequate reason, he would defend you in spite of the fact he disagreed with you. Once during one of our favorite outings—the Dodger baseball park—Nat was entertaining his business manager, Harold Plant, who happened to be a San Francisco Giants fan, and a music-publishing associate from out of town. When the out-of-town visitor heard Harold pulling for the Giants, he started to bait him rather loudly, in what most of us considered to be an attempt to butter up Nat. But suddenly Nat turned on the man and snapped, "Why don't you shut up! Harold's been a Giants fan since he was six years old, and he's not going to change for you or me or anybody."

It took quite a lot to arouse Nat, but once aroused, he could be a terror. Anything he cared for, he cared for deeply, and anything he didn't like he was much stronger against than most people realized. He was indeed a man of deep convictions. When really angered, which probably didn't happen more than a half-dozen times during our marriage, there was nothing to do but what I once told my sister, Charlotte, who happened to have been present during one of his rare outbursts. "The more you say, the worse you're going to make it," I warned her. "Let him blow it off. He'll get it all out of his system." And he always did.

His anger seldom lasted long, but it was magnificent during its moment. When Carlos Gastel once made the mistake during a party at our house of pressing the point that Nat was very susceptible to flattery—the truth if it was ever spoken—Nat got so angry with him that I had to turn out the lights on everybody. "The party's over," I announced.

At a big outdoor party around our pool one summer, guests milling about near Nat were surprised to hear him saying, "I hate that man. I hate that man." Almost no one had ever heard him speak that way about anybody. The man my husband was talking about turned out to be Orval Faubus, then Governor of Arkansas, who was defying the U.S. school desegregation laws. Nat had just seen television pictures of black children being cursed and spat upon as they tried to attend classes in Little Rock, and he could not contain himself.

But the only real feud I ever knew Nat to carry on was one with Harry Belafonte which was odd because Nat always had a lot of respect for Harry as a performer, and described him as one of the best.

But the two of them were sitting in a bar in Miami one night when Harry suddenly came up with what he considered to be a brilliant idea. "You aren't being presented right," Harry announced. "I'm going to sit down and write an act for you."

Nat listened to Harry for nearly half an hour, then told him, "I tell you what, Harry, you take care of Harry, I'll take care of Nat." But apparently Belafonte was not to be dissuaded so easily. He had big plans for Nat and wanted him to know it.

The evening finally reached the explosion point when Nat suddenly let Harry have it. "Look, I don't have to take off my clothes and bare my chest to sing calypso, because I was singing calypso before you. [Nat had recorded "Calypso Blues" back in 1949.] I'm a performer: a musician first, a singer second. You leave my act alone and I'll leave your act alone. I don't think I'm to the point where I need 'Harry Belafonte presents Nat King Cole.'"

I was in bed in our hotel when Nat came in and slammed the door. I jumped straight up. He was cursing like a sailor. All of a sudden I was glad I hadn't been there because I would have been blamed for the whole thing. All that Nat didn't tell me about, Sparky filled me in on later, because he had been at the bar with them.

Later, I think it hurt Nat that there was somebody he was angry with. And it certainly wasn't that in his heart Nat didn't like Harry. It was just that Belafonte had hurt him with his arrogance.

11

Parents and children and the problems inherent in that relationship are the same the world over, and neither class nor economic status changes anything much. Nat Cole was certainly a devoted, sometimes overgenerous, occasionally lackadaisical and, rarely, frustrated father.

We took the children with us everywhere we went when they were not in school, so they never knew insecurity. When they were in school, I would come home periodically and spend two or three weeks.

The first eight years we were married, Nat traveled an awful lot, but after that it wasn't so bad.

Once, when Cookie and Sweetie were still quite small, we went to the Cal-Veda Lodge in Tahoe, Nevada, for one of Nat's engagements. One morning, in a typical parental agreement, I asked Nat to keep an eye on the girls while I went shopping. Nat was rehearsing that day, so he took the kids into the show room with him.

When I returned, I went and checked with Nat to see where they were.

"They're back there playing," he said, waving toward the back of the huge room.

I took a look and didn't see them and called to him, "They're not back here."

We asked some of the other people working with the rehearsal if they had seen the children, and no one had. In a few minutes, however, we located Cookie, who was eight at the time, and she said her sister was around playing somewhere.

We started looking, but no Sweetie. Pretty soon the band stopped rehearsing and all the musicians started looking. There was a big excavation project going on nearby, the whole place was sitting on a lake, and ou. four-year-old daughter is missing.

By now, Nat is getting a little nervous.

We went down to where they were excavating and asked the workmen if any of them had seen Sweetie. None of them had. I looked at all those great mounds of dirt they were moving around, and began to panic over the idea that my child might be covered up under one of them. I couldn't help but start screaming at Nat. "You're no good!" I yelled at him. "You're a father and you can't even watch your children."

Nat was already feeling bad enough because he knew he had said he would look after them.

We went back to the hotel and called the sheriff. He came, the cooks came out of the kitchen and pretty soon everybody in the hotel was looking. Then the Nevada State Highway Patrol joined in the search.

Four long, agonizing hours passed and then a telephone call came into the hotel. "I think I have Nat King Cole's little girl here at my house," a woman's voice said on the other end. "She's asleep now, but she got on the tram near the hotel and got off when we did and started playing with my little girl."

All the while we had been there at the lodge, Sweetie had been saying she wanted to go for a ride on the tram, but no one had paid any attention to her.

Since Nat and I were practically the only Negroes in the area at the time and his appearance at the Cal-Veda was well publicized, I suppose it made it easy to assume that Sweetie was our daughter. But when you lose a child that young, four hours is like four days, and it was a very harrowing experience for all of us.

Even so, as the years rolled on we decided that we wanted to expand our family. When Sweetie was just nine months old I had become pregnant again, but I miscarried during one of our trips to Europe.

With two girls already in the family, we naturally thought it was time to have a boy. We were both definitely against another girl. There was only one absolute answer. "Honey, why don't we just adopt a boy," I suggested to Nat when Sweetie was nine years old.

Nat's one-word reply, full of enthusiasm, was "Yeah!"

The application and searching process took nine months, and finally one morning we received a call from the adoption agency. "Mrs. Cole, we have a young gentleman over here that you might be interested in seeing," a woman at the agency said. "You don't have to take him, you understand. You get to see at least three children. But this boy seems to fit in with your family."

In that moment I experienced all of the natural natal sensations that I had heard an adoptive mother gets: pains in the stomach, nausea. I walked back into the dining room and told the rest of the family about the call. Nat couldn't finish his breakfast, the girls got all excited and none of us could get out of the house fast enough.

I will never forget what a beautiful, sunshiny day it was outside.

At the agency, they brought the five-month-old boy into the room and he looked up at us with his big black eyes. I took him in my arms and Nat leaned over and looked at him, then they put him on the floor and Cookie and Sweetie played with him.

In a few minutes, Nat got up and said, "Okay, let's go."

"But, Mr. Cole," the adoption agency woman said in surprise, "aren't you going to. . . ."

"There's nothing to discuss," Nat cut in. "I've made my decision. I want him."

"Mr. Cole, I think you should spend a little more time with him," the woman persisted.

"Lady," Nat said firmly, "give me my child. This is the one we want, right, Skeez?"

I told him Yes, he was.

Later, when we got home, I began to worry a bit because we hadn't asked anything about him. I called my doctor and told him I needed a pediatrician right away because I had just adopted a child.

But I think Kelly must have been put here on earth for us to adopt. He is such a good, kind and intelligent boy, and I think Nat found something in Kelly that he missed as a boy. The two of them once spent the weekend at Disneyland without me, which both of them thoroughly enjoyed.

But when Nat took Kelly to a baseball game and Kelly didn't care for it, his father, who must have ranked some-

ABOVE Nat Cole at the age of 12 (*see arrow*) holding turkey won in Bud Billikin Day Contest.

BELOW The original Nat Cole Trio, with Oscar Moore on guitar and Wesley Prince on bass.

ABOVE Nat and Maria Cole at reception which followed their wedding in 1947. At left is Nat's mother.

LEFT Nat and Maria during the early days of their marriage.

ABOVE Nat King Cole playing the clavietta, an Italian wind instrument, at the Sands Hotel in Las Vegas.

LEFT Nat was a star attraction at the Sands for more than a decade.

LEFT Nat with son, Kelly, at Disneyland.

BELOW Nat as a surprised guest on *This Is Your Life* TV show in the late fifties. Around him are family and close friends, including: (*front row*) Glenn Wallichs, president of Capitol Records, Maria, daughters Natalie and Carol (Sweetie and Cookie); (*second row*) guitarist Oscar Moore, Nat's father Rev. E. J. Coles, his sister Evelyn Cole, his brother Eddie Cole and manager Carlos Gastel. In the back row, second from right is Bob Lewis, owner of the Swannee Inn, the first club in which the Nat Cole Trio appeared; and fourth from left is trio's original bassist, Wesley Prince. Remaining members of group in back row are members of Nat's Chicago high school band.

LEFT   Nat with President John F. Kennedy at a Los Angeles dinner in honor of the President in 1961 at the Hollywood Palladium.

BELOW   The King meets the Queen during a command performance for Queen Elizabeth in London during the early fifties.

OPPOSITE PAGE   Nat posing beside the rarely photographed
"Mona Lisa" at the Louvre.

ABOVE   A cluster of stars on a Hollywood movie lot, including:
Tony Curtis with camera, Nat, Peter Lawford approaching from
rear, and Frank Sinatra.

Nat King Cole playing the piano and relaxing on the set of *China Gate*, a film in which he co-starred.

where among the ten leading baseball fans in the world, was bitterly disappointed. "When I take him again, it'll be when he asks me," Nat fumed that day when they were back home.

But Kelly never cared for baseball, perhaps because he saw it as something that consumed such a large part of his father's interest, and therefore took time away from their relationship. Once, when Kelly was about three years old, Nat and I had come in off the road only to dash right out to the ball park for a Los Angeles Dodgers home game. The game was tied at the end of nine innings and ended up being one of those long, drawn-out affairs. Kelly was at home with his Aunt Barba (the children's name for Charlotte), who was listening to the game on radio and pulling for the Dodgers to get a hit. Suddenly Kelly blurted out, "Come on *anybody* and get a hit so my mommy and daddy can come home."

The birth of the twins in 1961 rounded out our family, and seemed to almost bring a new dimension to our lives. For one thing, it marked one of the few times in our marriage when Nat became completely uninhibited in his expression of love for me.

Despite the way my husband could sing a sentimental ballad and cast a romantic spell over millions of people in rooms large and small all around the world, he was not, in his private life, what one would call an expressive lover. Sometimes, when he was rehearsing, he would play songs and look at me and ask, "Do you like this one?" and I could tell from the way he was looking at me when he was singing that he was really singing the words to me. But he could rarely just say them, the way I could look at him and say, "I love you so much, honey." He could really write it better than he could say it, and I was disappointed that he didn't write more often, because he always expressed his affection in his letters. Otherwise, all his life he had difficulty expressing himself except within his music.

But even in simple, quick little notes he dashed off, he was romantic. I remember one he sent from St. Louis via special delivery back in 1951, when I must have been having trouble finding a housekeeper or something. It read:

"Hi, Sweetheart. Just a little note to say hello. I sure will be glad to get home because I miss you and the kids like mad. I really enjoyed talking to you last night because you sounded a lot happier. I guess so, because you found someone to relieve you of the pressure and I'm glad too. I guess when you get this letter it will be all over . . . Take care of yourself and kiss the kids for me. I love you. Nat. P.S. Forgive the pencil, I don't have a pen."

The details of the occasion are lost in my memory, but Nat's thoughtfulness remains with me in that letter.

That was the Nat Cole who expressed himself so openly when Casey and Timolin were born. I wasn't particularly thrilled over the idea of being pregnant. Oh, I had been delighted when I had Sweetie, first baby and all. But when a week before the twins were born the doctor told me it was going to be a double birth, I went through a thing.

First of all, Nat was scheduled to leave for Canada and I was pessimistic about that. I was sure he would be gone before I went to the hospital. He insisted he would not and, as it turned out, he was right.

"Have two fat ones," Nat called to me as they were rolling me off to the delivery room.

The delivery, however, was not easy. Certain complications developed, and it seemingly became problematical as to whether all of the lives involved could be saved. When Nat was told of the difficulty, he answered like a shot. "I don't give a damn," he said. "Save my wife."

Our attorney's wife was at the hospital and took a nurse aside and declared, "I know the rules of a Catholic hospital such as this. If there is a decision to be made, you always save the child. Well, Mrs. Cole is not Catholic."

"We're aware of that," the nurse replied.

In the end, we were all okay, and it was when Nat walked into the recovery room that it all came out. "Oh, honey, I love you," he cried.

"It was so hard, Nat," I murmured. "I tried to have boys."

"I don't care," Nat said. "You gave me two beautiful little girls, and I love you so much."

It was a beautiful moment and I still cherish its memory.

Yet a few days later, Nat displayed a completely opposite lack of perception during a sensitive moment. On the fourth day after the delivery, I came down with postnatal blues; and by that time Nat had gone on to Canada. He called me from there, and I cried as I talked to him on the phone. My friend Hannah was there in the room at the time; and when she took the phone from me, Nat asked, "What's the matter with Skeez?"

"She just wants you," Hannah told him.

Hannah gave the phone back to me as I wiped my tears and Nat again became sweet and sympathetic and loving. "Oh, honey, I'm so sorry I'm up here," he told me.

Nat named one of our twins Casey after baseball celebrity Casey Stengel, and Johnny Burke, the songwriter, who was our good friend, gave us the unusual name of Timolin for our other little girl.

Of all the children, however, Cookie, as our first child,

maintained a special place in Nat's heart. He did not live to see her begin her own career in show business as a stage and screen actress—and I am sure he would have been greatly pleased at the way critics have received her performances—but Nat was as proud as any father could be when Cookie was presented to Los Angeles Society by the city's Links Chapter in 1961.

The debutantes' ball, given at the Beverly Hilton Hotel, had to share the evening with a dinner given at the Hollywood Palladium in honor of President John F. Kennedy, where Nat also had to appear. Nat made his appearance on the dais with President Kennedy, whom we greatly admired and whom we came to regard as a personal friend, and doubled back to the hotel to bring Cookie out on his arm with the other fathers and daughters at the ball.

Nat had spoken to President Kennedy about Cookie's debut, and it was sometime after the grand presentation had been made that a secret service agent came into the ballroom and over to our table to speak privately to Nat. The two of them left the room together.

A few minutes later, bearing down on the ballroom with the full majesty of a naval armada, President Kennedy, Nat, and a platoon of secret service people swept in. The President greeted all of the debs and gave his special congratulations to Cookie, who admitted later that she thought she was going to faint.

Mr. Kennedy said, "It is the least that an itinerant President can do to repay a favor Nat King Cole has just done for me by appearing at my dinner."

It was an exciting, memorable and glorious evening for the entire Cole family.

12

It was the day before Easter Sunday in 1953, and in a few hours Nat and I would be celebrating our fifth wedding anniversary. We had a dinner date that evening with our friend Ivan Mogull.

Nat had to do a television show that afternoon, and the next day would mark the start of a thirty-day tour of "The Big Show of 1953," which he himself would be sponsoring in partnership with Carlos Gastel, with an opening at Carnegie Hall.

Ivan and I were waiting at the Warwick Hotel for Nat to return.

Meanwhile, having left the television studio, Nat and Sparky were walking up Sixth Avenue. It was near six in the evening, and just beginning to get dark.

As they walked, Nat suddenly began to tire, and then, leaning his six-foot frame down on Sparky, told him: "I feel dizzy."

By the time they reached the corner, with Sparky helping him along, Nat said suddenly, "My stomach is killing me!"

Sparky started hailing a cab just as a light rain began to fall. Momentarily, a taxi pulled to within three feet of the curb and Sparky opened the door. The driver took one look at Sparky's brown face and snapped, "I'm off duty!"

"I've got a sick man here," Sparky said quickly.

"I don't give a goddamn, I'm off duty," the cab driver declared.

My husband, wincing with pain, was shoved bodily into the cab as Sparky told him, "Come on, Nat, get in the cab!" Then to the driver, Sparky snarled, "I don't give a goddamn what you say, I've got a sick man here. Take me to the Warwick Hotel!"

The driver looked back and saw Nat sitting with his head leaning back. "Oh, Nat King Cole," he said in recognition. As he drove he began to explain that his family had all of Nat's records. God only knows what that driver would have done had it been any other black man sick in the street.

The attack had subsided by the time they reached the hotel, and they told me nothing of the incident or of the fact that during rehearsals that day Nat had vomited up blackened blood in a bathroom.

The next day, with Nat having to work that evening, we spent a good part of our anniversay being happily lazy together at the Warwick. By that night, as we arrived at the hall, Nat suddenly felt dizzy as he started up the stairs, and then he went into the bathroom and vomited blood again. Ivan immediately called a physician friend of his, Dr. Jerry Lieberman. After examining Nat, Dr. Lieberman warned, "I won't be responsible if you go on that stage."

"Well, at least let me go out and tell the people," Nat said. Then he went out and explained to the audience that he was ill and a doctor in the wings forbade his appearance.

An ambulance was called to take Nat directly to a hospital, the very thought of which seemed to frighten him tremendously. "You know, I've never been to a hospital before," Nat said to Carlos, who rode with us.

"You'll be all right," Carlos tried to assure him.

"Yeah, but I've never been to a hospital before," Nat repeated.

"Look," Carlos said patiently, "you've got a good doctor, they know what you've got and they know they can get at it and you'll get the best of care."

As if in a trance, Nat said for the third time, "Yeah, but I've never been in a hospital before."

Nat's problem was bleeding ulcers, and apparently he had been ignoring some stomach problems for a long time. The attack was the first I had heard of.

Nat was in the hospital for three weeks before undergoing surgery. Meanwhile, I had consultation after consultation with doctors, and an operation was recommended. Some people wanted me to move Nat to another hospital where a very well-known doctor was associated. But one of the five doctors consulted, Dr. Halpern, a personal friend, who had given us blood tests when we were married, called me and said: "Maria, the head surgeon here is one of the finest in the country. It not only would be embarrassing to the hospital if you were to move Nat, but it is really not necessary. I do recommend that you operate because with Nat traveling like he does, who knows, he might get down there in one of those Southern towns and have an attack and bleed to death because some hospital won't take him."

I sat there all morning with some friends during the surgery in which the doctors removed part of Nat's stomach. Finally, Dr. Nelson Cornell came out and told me, "He's as strong as a bull, Maria. There's not another thing wrong with him."

It's strange, but I remember having a slight fear of cancer, even in those days when you didn't worry as much about it as you do now.

The doctors wouldn't let Nat smoke for three months, and all that time he did not touch a cigarette. The very day the three-month period ended, he started smoking again.

Meanwhile, after the operation, Nat came home to recuperate.

Everything was going along fine when suddenly Nat somehow managed to eat some tainted food, possibly something that had been frozen, thawed and refrozen. What I know for certain is that Nat turned green and this time we really thought he was going to die. We rushed him to a hospital where soon, as my sister Charlotte recalls, "They had a tube everywhere they could get a tube."

But Nat's constitution was strong, perhaps too strong, for the experience of the ulcer attack was a sign to all of us that my husband preferred to endure a great deal of pain in silence rather than complain; and this tendency, in the end, would hurt him far, far more than it would help.

13

The pain of bodily illness was not the only one my husband learned to endure. Nat's fame as an entertainer had now spread far and wide, and with it had grown his reputation as a human being. You could hear it again and again: from fellow performers, club and theater owners, business associates and fans. And it was always the same, "He's a real gentleman, one of the finest people I've ever met."

There was but one catch: this fine, talented gentleman happened to be a black man. While millions paid to hear him sing and thousands rushed for his autograph, at meal or bedtime he was often an unwelcomed guest.

One of the earliest incidents occurred before our marriage on Nat's first venture into Las Vegas. He was offered $4,500 a week to play the Thunderbird Hotel. Being white, Nat's road manager, Mort Ruby, was offered a suite at the hotel for free during their engagement. Meanwhile, as Mort told it later, "I had to go by cab to find Nat a place in the dirtiest, filthiest hole I had ever seen in my life. It was absolutely heartbreaking. I finally located a motel on the other side

of the tracks, where the woman had the nerve to charge
Nat $15 a day.

The star of the Thunderbird's show could not go into the
hotel gambling casino, or anywhere else in the hotel, except
for a sitting room that was fixed up adjoining the kitchen.
Nat decided then and there he would never play Las Vegas
again unless conditions were changed.

The change came two years later when my husband, as
quietly as it was kept, broke the color line in Las Vegas.
Beldon Katleman, one of the few sole owners of a strip
hotel there, wanted the trio, and Carlos Gastel told Beldon
exactly how it had to be. "We will work it, providing Nat
and the boys can live, eat, gamble, drink or whatever they
want to do on the premises of the El Rancho Vegas, without any prejudice shown against them whatsoever."

"You've got it," Beldon agreed.

Haggling over price on a later occasion, however, caused
Nat to break another rule in Vegas. When Beldon Katleman asked for a return engagement by the trio, at only a
slightly higher figure than the first time, Carlos told him,
"Look, Beldon, we accomplished what we wanted to the
first time and everything was okay, but now we gotta get
paid. We proved to everybody in town that there was no
problem. Now I would like to have what this man is worth."

There was an agreement among the Las Vegas hotel
owners at that time that an entertainer couldn't play another place within a year of the conclusion of an engagement, and that no owner would solicit an act within that
time. This was in an effort to stop the pirating of name acts
by one club from another. Beldon Katleman, knowing this
to be the case, refused to raise his offering price for the

Nat King Cole Trio and suggested that Carlos might try to find work for them "up the street."

Carlos left Katleman and went up to Lake Tahoe where the group was appearing that week, and Jack Entratter, who had just come out to Las Vegas to take over the Sands Hotel, and whom Carlos had known in New York, flew up to Tahoe to discuss having the trio work for him. "We'll come and work for you, but you've got a problem on your hands," Carlos told him. "You got this rule that you cannot solicit an act that's played another club in Vegas during the past year."

Jack Entratter answered, "Look, I came out here to get this place moving and to fill up that room. I don't care about any boy-scout rules they've got here or anything else. If you want to play it, I'll give you a contract and you come in and play it."

The group accepted the contract, and that was the beginning of a lifelong deal between Nat and the Sands. For a time after that, Beldon Katleman barred both Carlos and Tom Rockwell of General Artists Corporation, the trio's booking agency, from the premises of the El Rancho.

All turned out not to be sweetness and light at the Sands, however. During their preshow rehearsal, Nat told his crew that they could sign their names at the hotel's Garden Room for meals and would receive a discount on their bills. But at the Garden Room they found their way barred by the maître d', who informed them they could not be served there. Sparky went back and found Nat lacing on a tie in the dressing room with a few people around.

After the situation was presented, Nat told Sparky, "Get Jack Entratter on that phone right now."

Harold Dobrow, the Sands stage manager and one of those present, was unaware of Nat's arrangement with Jack Entratter, and nervously began to try to explain the problem of serving Negroes in the hotel.

"If you don't get Jack Entratter in five minutes, I'm packing up and getting the hell out of here," Nat declared flatly.

The room began to clear of people.

Entratter appeared shortly, asking what the matter was.

"What about my fellows eating downstairs?" Nat demanded.

"Of course they can," Entratter replied.

"Well, call those bastards down there and tell 'em," Nat said.

Jack went down and straightened the matter out in nothing flat.

Nat also encountered trouble at hotels where he was not playing. The Sahara Hotel, for instance, was also interested in Nat as a performer, and some overtures had been made to him. Nat was even given the impression that his presence was welcome in the club at any time. He went in one evening with a group of five or six others and they all had drinks and talked at the bar, without incident.

The next evening, having decided to take in one of the Sahara's lounge acts, Nat and some friends went over again. This time a security guard stopped Nat at the door and told him he could not enter. Nat, surprised and embarrassed, asked for the club's manager, Bill Miller, who had been discussing the possibility of Nat's appearing there. Mr. Miller, Nat was informed, was in an important meeting and couldn't come down to see about the situation. It was two o'clock in the morning.

"Well," Nat said angrily when he got back to his own hotel, "cancel them out—completely."

Nat never played the Sahara Hotel.

He called me after the incident. He was deeply hurt and he turned to me as he always did in such times. I would have been angry enough to burn the place down, but that was not Nat's way. Yet, anybody who thinks Nat Cole was an Uncle Tom didn't know the man. Nat was treated royally at the Desert Inn, even though the hotel then maintained a policy of barring Negroes. But my husband decided he would have none of it. "Okay, so they're nice," he explained. "But I don't want them. I can't use them. They're good to me, but what about the other guy who comes in there and happens to be Negro?"

As quiet as it was kept, Nat sometimes anticipated trouble, not for himself, but for other black people who wished to see him perform. At the Chez Paree in Chicago, for instance, back when Negro patrons at the top-priced nightclubs were still a rarity, Nat told the owners, "Now look, I don't want to see all the Negroes put in the back of the room in here."

They told him, "Anybody who comes in here will be treated as a human being, and if you see anything wrong, or hear of it, you can walk right off the stage."

Nat promised he would do just that.

In the early days, unfortunately, many Negroes were unaware of the subtleties of tipping the maître d' in order to get a good table in the plush clubs. Nat made up for this in part by always tipping stage hands and presenting a gift to the maître d' at the end of his engagements. Often when he returned to the club later, he would notice a different seating policy for Negroes.

Ofttimes he would just simply say to a club owner over a drink, "I see you're putting all the Negroes in left field. What is this?" The next night he would look out and there would be a change. He knew how to pick his times for this, too. He always said, "When you're doing business in a nightclub, the boss is your friend. If business is no good, don't bother him."

Such incidents as those in Las Vegas were not uncommon by any means. In June of 1946, the trio played The Lookout House in Covington, Kentucky, where Mort Ruby was summoned into the manager's office as the trio was unloading their gear outside.

"You the road manager of this group?" the man demanded.

"Yes, I am," Mort told him.

"I have some mail for you from the GAC office," the club manager told Mort. Then he added, "Sit down, I want to talk to you for a minute. There are a few things I want to tell you and I want you to convey my message to your group."

"Like what?" Mort asked.

"Like under no circumstances are they to go anywhere but backstage," the man said. "They are not allowed in the club, in the restaurant, in the gambling rooms, or in the bar ever. And if I see you—you're a Jew, aren't you?"

"Yes, I am," Mort answered.

"If I see you or any of those others in any of those places," the club manager continued, "I'm going to shoot you."

With that he reached down into his desk drawer and pulled out a .45 caliber automatic.

That was one of the longest one-week engagements the Nat King Cole Trio ever spent anywhere.

Mort never told Nat of the gun-pulling incident, and, since there were no witnesses to the conversation, Mort did not feel they could break the engagement. Other members of the club's staff gently explained to the trio that their presence anywhere in the club except onstage should be avoided.

Nightclubs were certainly not the only source of trouble. Once coming out of Springfield, Illinois, into Chicago, Mort wired ahead to the Bismarck Hotel for reservations for Nat and me. When we arrived at the hotel and started up the marble steps, Mort could feel a cold sweat (as he described it later) as if something were going to happen. Inside, he went to the desk to check us in and pick up the room key; and the hotelman suddenly declared, "I'm sorry, but I don't have your reservation."

Mort then produced a telegram from the hotel confirming our reservation and the hotelman tried to grab it from him.

"Do we get a room or don't we?" Mort demanded, holding on to the wire.

Grudgingly the hotelman told us to wait in the lobby, and after a long while a room was made available, but not a very good room. In fact, we often found ourselves being shuttled into hotel salesrooms and other cubbyholes, such as at the Ben Franklin in Philadelphia. Of course, sometimes we were unable to get rooms at all, and this was the basis for lawsuits in a few places like Rock Island, Illinois, and Pittsburgh where, after we were told there were no rooms available at the Mayfair Hotel, Nat sent our white bongo player, Jack Costanza, in to request a room and he was given one.

It had not been too difficult to avoid trouble of this sort in Dixie. In those days, segregation was the law of the Southland, and this was taken into account during any plans we made for appearing there. The group would travel on a large passenger bus on which alternate rows of seats had been removed to provide more room, and food was taken aboard at selected stops, often by white members of the troupe. Lodging would be secured at homes of prominent black members of the community. With precaution, insults could be avoided, and Nat traveled with a reasonable degree of security. Furthermore, as Nat's prominence grew, he curtailed most Southern travel.

Nevertheless, in other and far broader ways racial prejudice hampered my husband's brilliant career, limiting his success in such areas as radio and television.

Nat's brief radio career happened quite by accident. He had started making guest appearances on the Kraft Music Hall early in 1946, and in October of that year did his first show for Wildroot Cream Oil. Woody Herman's orchestra had recorded the Wildroot theme in a fast tempo and somebody—probably Walt Maurer, a fan of Nat's, who was advertising manager at Wildroot and wrote songs and jingles, including the Wildroot theme, and later became company president—got the idea that it would be cute if Nat did a singing commercial.

Nat was in Philadelphia at the Earl Theater, and arrangements were made to go to a radio station and cut a few samples. Nat did the "Wildroot Cream Oil Charlie" theme in a medium tempo and it was a success. From then on, NBC would pick up the trio every Saturday afternoon in whatever town they were in for a weekly, thirty-minute broadcast that included some of the top guest stars in the business.

The show also had a few guests who, at the time, were not household names. Once when Jo Stafford was unable to make a Los Angeles guest spot due to last-minute illness, Mort Ruby recruited a singer he heard about who was appearing at a club across the street from the NBC studios at Sunset and Vine. After the show, Mort presented him with the usual one-hundred-dollar payment, considered only a token fee for the big names, and told him, "Here, go buy yourself some ties." The singer was Frankie Lane, who in greener years aboard a plane en route from Canada to New York reminded Mort of the incident. "Only I didn't buy ties," Frankie said, "I bought some tires."

Nat's *Wildroot Cream Oil Show* was good enough to last four years.

Television was a different story, however. Again, Nat was a first, the first black person to have a network TV show, but it was a very hard row to hoe.

Nat was interested in doing television right from the beginning. It was a question of wanting to prove himself, and when the industry started going for big-name musical talent, there was no reason why—except for the question of color—my husband should not have been one of the first considered.

But to the industry, color seemed to be the only consideration.

Everyone connected with the industry was alerted to the fact that Nat was available, but nothing was forthcoming. It finally got to the point where Nat and Carlos notified GAC that the booking agency's contract would not be renewed unless a television deal was made. As Carlos put it, "I don't think we're being outrageous about it or too demanding, because although we know what problem they're having, we have given them a lot of time, and we figure it's time for them to force something, even at the expense of maybe alienating a business relationship."

One of the disgusting parts about the whole affair was that everybody pretended to be so polite about it. What people really felt and what you were told were two different things. In discussing it business-wise, nobody ever came right out and said, "Well, the man is black and you can't get him on TV." Among close friends it was discussed, of course, but generally the excuses given were that they didn't have enough time, or that there wasn't enough money.

As far as the sales people were concerned, there wasn't anybody going out and pitching a Negro on a show because that wasn't the easiest thing to sell. A saleman wants to make a sale, and the average one doesn't care what he's selling as long as he can sell it quickly. A black star was no quick sale.

Fortunately, some good men were trying to break the barrier. GAC President Tom Rockwell was working on the problem in New York, where NBC wanted Perry Como, and Tom was trying to present a combination deal including Nat.

Carlos was in the West Coast offices of GAC in Los Angeles one day discussing the problem when the phone rang. It was Harold Kemp, who was in charge of programming at NBC on the West Coast. He had an offer. "We just had a cancellation on Frankie Carlyle," he explained. "I'm going to try to sell it to New York for you guys. Come on over here and we'll talk about it."

The *Frankie Carlyle Show* wasn't any prime time block-buster. It was fifteen minutes in the late afternoon. But to Nat fifteen minutes of television was fifteen minutes of television, and here again was the challenge of setting a precedent and proving that a black man was acceptable.

The actual problems were many: there was hardly enough money for anything but a band, everything was paid for at scale—or minimum—prices, and Nat's schedule of personal appearances had to be arranged so that he could spend a certain number of weeks in New York, and Hollywood or some other locale where there were facilities to do a telecast, for he could hardly afford to give up his other work for a show for which he would not get paid. His personal earnings from TV went back into production costs.

It was hard to tell just how well those fifteen-minute shows were doing, but when summer came, Nat was given a half-hour prime time spot. Now he had more freedom, more money and more facilities. Still, it was tough. The show was built around guest stars, which meant people like Peggy Lee, Kay Starr, the Mills Brothers, Ella Fitzgerald and scores of other top names came to work for only a couple of hundred dollars. Even Harry Belafonte, whose television price was so high almost nobody could afford him, came to work on Nat's show for scale.

Sponsors were slow forming up, but NBC was willing to carry the show for a while. The South, of course, reared up in self-indignation. Many Southern stations either never carried the show or else soon dropped it. The reaction was almost insane. One station manager confided, "I like Nat Cole, but they told me if he came back on, they would bomb my house and my station."

Nevertheless, TV stations in some seventy-seven cities

around the country did carry the Nat Cole Show, and it got both high ratings and critical acclaim. NBC put virtually its entire sales staff to work on the problem of lining up sponsors, and although the show was figured to be worth $86,650 per week, it was offered to advertisers at a total cost of $45,000.

One of the reasons NBC could offer it so cheaply was that Nat was working at a fraction of his normal fee. His usual price for a TV guest appearance at that time was $7,500, yet he was working on his own show for $1,500. During the sixty weeks the show eventually ran, the money Nat lost from giving up nightclub engagements, including lucrative Las Vegas salaries, represented a tremendous financial sacrifice.

Some sponsorship did trickle in, but the big money failed to materialize. As one advertising agency man put it, apparently expressing Madison Avenue's attitude at the time, "I think Nat could do a fine sales job on a product. Somebody ought to buy him. My outfit won't because things are considered too fluid down South."

The word was the same almost all over. I never will forget Carlos walking into Nat's dressing room during one of those depressing periods of trying to line up top sponsors and announcing, "Max Factor's people say no Negro can sell lipstick for him."

Without the big money, the Nat Cole Show could not hope to survive in prime time. NBC began to shift the program about, into earlier and earlier time slots. Finally, Harold Kemp summoned Carlos in and said, "I've got some news for you. They're going to put this show on at seven o'clock on Saturday nights."

Carlos said: "Good-bye, Harold."

Carlos went back to Nat, who was rehearsing for a telecast that evening. "Seven o'clock Saturday night is cowboy time," Carlos complained.

"So what did you do?" Nat asked.

"We quit," his manager replied. "We're through in two weeks."

And so in December of 1957, Nat telecast his last show. He was hurt and angry, for he knew he had done a good job, even occasionally beating out the top-rated $64,000 Question, which at that time was trouncing everybody.

For all of his excellence, showmanship and talent, Nat Cole was still a black man, and in 1957, television was still the white man's world.

Nat, himself, put it best when he explained his TV demise. "Madison Avenue," he said, "is afraid of the dark."

14

It would be a long time before Nat Cole would lose his
anger over the forces that caused him to abandon television.
Certainly he had been the victim of a personal kind of race
prejudice before, but now the insult was to his talent and
professionalism as a performer. The television networks were
afraid of the sponsors, he declared, and the sponsors, in
turn, were frightened out of their wits by a few negative
letter-writers, ignoring the vast majority of Americans who
may have felt differently.

"Sponsors don't have any guts," Nat said flatly. "They
pay far, far too much attention to cranks. There may be a
hundred thousand who like a performance given by a Negro
on TV, and maybe not one of them writes in. And then
maybe one crank writes in that uh-uh, he doesn't like that
Nigra boy, and the whole sponsor's economy gets panicky."

Four years after the end of his own television show, Nat
told newsman Murray Schumach of *The New York Times*,
"Some of the worst bigots in the country have my records.
There is a lot more integration in the actual life of the

United States than you will find on television. I notice they always had integration in the prison scenes."

Nat had just finished doing a spectacular for the Canadian Broadcasting Corporation, and recalled that his own failure on American TV had come despite his own efforts and those of some of the biggest entertainment names in the world, who had waived their usual salaries to work for him. The system worked against them all, Nat declared.

"I'm not just talking about myself," my husband told Schumach, "and it is not just the money. I made an enormous sum last year from my records and nightclub dates. You take a Negro like Dick Gregory. All the critics say he is great. Television will give Joey Bishop a show and Bob Newhart a show. But they won't give Dick Gregory a show. He's a Negro and he does guest appearances."

The problem was not the fault of show business, Nat said. "Real show people are democratic. All performers have one thing in common, they understand talent and they appreciate talent. The trouble is with the people who run show business. The people who are in charge of the television industry are not a part of that show business. The trouble is that the people who run these shows do the thinking for the American people before the people get a chance themselves."

Remembering the cosmetics company's remark about Negroes not selling its product, Nat snorted, "What do they think we use? Chalk? Congo paint? And what about corporations like the telephone company? A man sees a Negro on a television show. What's he going to do, call up the telephone company and tell them to take out his telephone?"

Nat's criticisms may seem harsh and antiquated in this era when black people like Bill Cosby, Diahann Carroll and Leslie Uggams have had their own TV shows, and almost every other prime time show you see has a Negro featured, but this has all happened virtually overnight. When one realizes that Nat spoke less than ten years ago —only four years before his death—one realizes how long the iron fist of racial prejudice had remained clenched, and how it dogged my husband all his life.

In this new age of enlightenment, Nat could have quite conceivably been one of the major luminaries of the television screen, but it is possible he would not have wanted that distinction. A few years after he was off the air, he admitted, "I wanted a series of my own badly, and I got one, and I'm glad I had one when I did. But right now, I wouldn't want to do a series again. A singer on TV learns his lessons. A straight singing series just won't hold up. Even a singing variety show can give you exposure trouble. That over-exposure bit has to get everybody who sings on TV. On TV, if you're emcee and also the performing star, you've got problems of how to last. A non-performing star emcee like Ed Sullivan can last forever. He introduces the acts and gets out of the way."

In these observations, Nat was extremely prophetic. Singing stars who stuck with it, like Dinah Shore and Perry Como, finally had to throw in the towel, while Ed Sullivan kept rolling like the Mississippi River.

But Nat also saw the changes coming in opportunities for black performers. "The future looks very good," he told Gene Grove in an interview for the *New York Post*. "The agencies and the networks are not so concerned with color as they were. I think things are going to improve tremendously. Attitudes have changed and even Madison Avenue has to keep up with the times."

As always when Nat became angry, he had to be severely provoked, and his earlier blasts at television would never have been made had the situation not been rotten to the core. "I'm a performer, not a professional agitator," Nat explained to Grove. "I don't believe in lip service. I'm not for talking, criticizing, blasting. I'm interested in doing something positive."

With then only eleven months to live, almost to the day, Nat gave what was perhaps his best summation of his matured philosophy. "We're all always, of course, aware of race, but I'm not bitching. *Life* is a bitch. People look at me and I'm doing all right and a lot of people have a lot less than I do and they could say, 'What are you bitching about?' If I'm fighting at all, I'm fighting for the cause of man."

15

The kind of racial sickness that was America's (and often still is) reached its physical zenith as far as my husband was concerned on the night of April 10, 1956, in his home state of Alabama.

On a Southern tour of one-nighters, Nat was bringing an integrated show to much of Dixie for the first time. On the bill with him was the late Ted Heath and his band, singer June Christie, the Four Freshmen, and comedian Gary Morton. In its first week on the tour, the show had grossed $110,000.

The seating pattern of the audiences varied from city to city on that tour. In San Antonio, Mexican-Americans, blacks and whites all sat side by side. In Fort Worth, the audience had been split down the middle, half black, half white. The same was true in Houston, except there a few of the overflowing crowd of Negroes were seen spotted among the white section. In Winston-Salem, no one seemed to care that the audience was racially mixed.

But in segregationist Alabama, native son or no native

son, Nat had to perform for completely segregated audiences. Seven thousand people turned out in Mobile, Alabama, the night before Birmingham. Now on April 10, in Birmingham, Nat was to render two peformances: the first for an all-white audience, the second for Negroes only.

But the setting for the more dramatic events of that evening were laid not by booking agents or show promoters or the performers themselves, but by a small group of men four days earlier at a gasoline station, sixty-five miles from Birmingham. The scheme, concocted by members of the town's White Citizens' Council and shocking in its absurd audacity, called for a mob of one hundred whites to descend upon the Birmingham Municipal Auditorium, infiltrate the audience at a given moment, overpower the band, police and anyone else who dared to interfere, and forcibly kidnap Nat King Cole.

When the night arrived, however, only six men in a car loaded with rifles, brass knuckles and blackjacks came to the auditorium. The first show—for the white audience—was well underway when the men made their move. Nat had come on as the starring act, and had just swung into the concluding lyrics of his third song, "Little Girl." Four men, apparently unnoticed, started for the stage. Nat, singing before a microphone at the stage's edge, suddenly heard a woman's scream cut through the auditorium, just as someone lunged over the footlights for his feet. The assailant's movement tripped over the microphone, which struck Nat flush in the face, and he toppled backward against the piano.

In an instant, the house was alive with action. Birmingham police, already alerted to watch for trouble because the area's White Citizens' Council groups had been urging

a boycott against Negro music as decadent, swarmed over
three of the intruders. The fourth man, having not reached
the stage with the others, apparently turned and fled when
the melee broke out.

The battle was fierce. A policeman had to smash his
nightstick against the head of one of the attackers to get
him to release his grip on Nat, while another of the assail-
ants broke an officer's nose with a soft-drink bottle.

Off in the wings, Sparky, who had been giving cues to
the lighting man, began to yell, "Close the curtains! Close
the curtains!" The curtain started to close but in the confusion they were opened again. Sparky and some of the
others rushed to help Nat off stage.

Meanwhile, an almost comic scene had developed. Nat's
drummer, Lee Young, started a drum roll and yelled for the
band to go into "The Star-Spangled Banner," which the
English band didn't know. Instead, they began playing their
own anthem, "God Save the Queen." Sparky was back yell-
ing, "Close the curtains" and "To hell with the Queen!"
The audience, by then, was on its feet, women were screaming, policemen were whipping heads and the guy who was
supposed to be closing the curtains was standing there
watching the fight.

When things finally settled down, the stunned band refused to play anymore. Nat came back to the stage, despite
his busted lip and aching back, and received a long ovation.
Obviously shocked, he told the audience, "I just came here
to entertain you. That was what I thought you wanted. I
was born here in Alabama. Those folks hurt my back. I
can't continue because I have to go to see a doctor."

Nat turned out to be all right physically, but the furor
that arose over the attack was to cause him mental anguish

for years. The six hoodlums were all arrested and convicted, something of a triumph itself for black victims of white attacks in those days, and Nat was complimented by the judge, who said my husband's conduct during the whole affair was such as to "win him new friends in the South." I, by nature more volatile in temperament than my husband, did not quite share his forbearance with some of the shameful acts which were committed against him, professionally and physically. For my part, there should have been hell to pay, but Nat was simply different.

In El Paso, disc jockey Johnny Miles of Station KELP began playing a marathon of Nat's recordings in tribute to him, and Police Chief Frank Littlejohn in Charlotte, North Carolina, begged Nat to come to his city and perform, guaranteeing him safety. Also in Charlotte, however, radio-TV announcer Bob Raiford was fired from his job after he denounced the attack on the air, and from other quarters criticism of Nat's having appeared before a segregated audience in the first place was heard.

A quick poll of other Negro show business people indicated most of them felt Nat shouldn't have appeared the way he did, and even Thurgood Marshall, who was then chief counsel for the NAACP, suggested that all Nat needed to complete his role as an Uncle Tom was "a banjo."

Why, indeed, was Nat Cole playing before segregated audiences? My husband explained it himself. "Those people, segregated or not, are still record fans," he told newsmen. "They can't overpower the law of the South, and I can't come in on a one-night stand and overpower the law. The whites come to applaud a Negro performer like the colored do. When you've got the respect of white and colored, you can erase a lot of things. I can't settle the issue. If I was that good, I should be President of the United States. But I can help to ease the tension by gaining the respect of both races all over the country."

The very fact that the seating pattern had varied so widely in cities throughout the South during his tour was evidence in itself that the country was changing, Nat felt, and furthermore some 3,500 people in Birmingham had come out to see the first show ever put on by black and white performers in the city.

"The important thing," said Nat, "is for Negroes and whites to communicate. Even if they sit on separate sides of the room, maybe at intermission a white fellow will ask a Negro for a match or something, and maybe one will ask the other how he likes the show. That way, you have started them to communicating, and that's the answer to the whole problem."

There were many who disagreed with Nat, especially when their great wisdom was enhanced by hindsight. But my husband by background and personality was never a violent and angry man. Indeed, most of the violent, angry black men of the sixties were nowhere in evidence in 1956. Times have changed; hatred and revenge would never have been Nat's reaction, then or now. He was not that kind of man. Nat sincerely believed in the inherent good and kindness of man, that good did indeed eventually triumph over evil, and in the Christian ethic of turning the other cheek.

Anybody who truly knew the kind of man my husband was and what he stood for would hardly have expected Nat to do anything other than what he did, nor would they have faulted him for doing it.

But a controversy over Nat Cole's racial posture had begun, and it would plague him for the rest of his life.

Immediately after the Birmingham incident, friends in Detroit tried to persuade Nat to fly to New York and publicly give his support to the NAACP.

"How many benefits have you done for the NAACP?" one asked Nat.

"I don't know," he replied.

"Well, why don't you write down a list of what you've done," it was suggested.

Nat declined. "Why should I?" he asked. "I didn't do it for publicity."

Nat had his own thoughts about doing things, as he expressed in a four-page letter (a rare feat, indeed, for him to write) to a woman who had protested his playing Australia because of its racist reputation. "If I can go down there and get these people to realize that we Negroes are human beings," Nat wrote, "and to accept us as we are today, then I will have helped to some degree."

When we sued a Rock Island, Illinois, hotel for refusing us accommodations, the case ended with the jury deadlocked on our $62,000 damage suit, but the hotel immediately adopted a policy of integration and Nat was satisfied. He hadn't brought the suit for the money involved. His satisfaction stemmed from the hotel's legally inspired decision to change its racial policy, which would affect the black John Does who might wish to stay there in the future.

But as late as 1963, the wolves were still howling at the door. Martin Luther King, Jr., was rallying Negroes in the South, and a few entertainers had joined in. Several Negro newspapers suddenly printed stories suggesting that Nat was holding himself removed from the emerging black revolution. It was so bad that Nat's attorney demanded an immediate retraction, pointing out that the stories were based on alleged interviews that never took place.

Nat, himself, could remain silent no longer. In a carefully worded but nevertheless angry retort, he told the public: "If I truly believed that my appearance in the South would help to cure—or even arrest—the cancerous evil of prejudice, I would not hesitate to go. I do not happen to believe this, and I presume that I am still permitted that privilege. I may applaud the courage of those entertainers who go to Alabama, but the suggestion that every prominent Negro who does not get on the first plane South is turning his back on his people is obviously both stupid and ridiculous."

Nat Cole, for all of his fame, was still a black man in a white world, and the white world had never let him forget that. "It is nothing short of impossible for the Negro entertainer to forget his origins," Nat declared.

Nat then voiced his support of the black movement. "The moral and spiritual guidance being furnished to our people and to our country by Reverend Martin Luther King, Jr., is to me the most significant and outstanding achievement of our time," he said. "What he and men like him are doing today is a matter of the deepest concern to me. But I choose to believe that it must be a matter of concern that calls for action not only from Negroes, certainly not only from people in the entertainment business, but from every thinking American interested in the future of our country."

Entertainers, Nat felt, could best help by giving time and money to raising funds to support "in a very specific financial way the work of men like Dr. King."

Having had his say, Nat then went out to put his money

where his mouth had been. He raised $50,000 for various civil rights groups, and he later helped raise nearly $130,000 in Los Angeles to fight an attempt to revoke California's antidiscrimination housing laws.

Nat was helping the best he knew how.

16

For a man of my husband's seemingly unlimited musical talent, it is an amazing omission in his career that he never made it big on Broadway. Nightclubs, motion pictures, television. . . . They all knew the Nat Cole charm.

It wasn't that Nat didn't want to play Broadway; it just happened that way. It certainly wasn't because he didn't try. In fact, in 1960, he went all out for it with a musical show called *I'm with You*. The show opened on the West Coast and traveled as far east as Detroit before the critics shot it down. Nat had put a lot of his own money into it, and Capitol Records made an investment too. But, besides helping to launch the career of Barbara McNair, who showed a decided talent for musical comedy, the show did little else.

Nat came up with a stage winner, however, although not for Broadway, with a show called *Sights and Sounds*. In three years, it played more than one hundred cities, and it was perhaps right that Nat would be so pleased with the vehicle in which he would make his last public appearance.

The show rolled through city after city from Los Angeles to Buffalo, N.Y.; and, the people really turned out: Easterners in their tuxes, Westerners in open-throated sport shirts, college kids in sweaters. *Sights and Sounds* played nightclubs, Greek theaters and tent-topped stages in the round.

The show was pure American. There was comedy, dancing and music all performed by a cast of a dozen bright and pert singers and dancers who did songs like "Buttons and Bows," "Lullaby of Broadway" and "Precious Lord." Holding it all together was Nat King Cole, singing the old favorites like "Paper Moon" and "Mona Lisa" together with the hits that had come twenty years later like "Rambling Rose." For the really sentimental oldtime Cole fans, he played some magnificent piano.

Nat first brought out *Sights and Sounds* for only six weeks in 1962, "just as a feeler," he said. It was successful enough for him to try it again in 1963. After that, Nat knew he had a hit on his hands.

As he started out what would be his last year, he was confident. "Last year, we really had success," he enthused, "and I really established myself as a concert artist. I'm happy I got into it now. We played last year in places where I have fans I never see—Detroit, Rochester, Minneapolis, places like that. I played nightclubs for a long while, and I sort of need the change mentally. Besides, I wanted to create a new image, so I'm performing before a vast new audience. They say only 40 percent of the people attend nightclubs. So, if I play New York City, I'm not performing for the people of New York, I'm playing for those comparative few who go to the Copacabana. Also, there are kids who can't go to nightclubs, but who can and do come to concerts."

Part of the showmanship that was Nat's lay in his understanding and anticipation of his audiences. "The audience is entirely different," he said in making a comparison with nightclub patrons. "These people are theatergoers; and, that's why I want to try something different every year. It's a different kind of atmosphere, so you have to create a different image. Too, concert audiences are a little more critical. They don't have liquor or food to distract them."

The success of *Sights and Sounds*, like all of the other successes in Nat's life, did not come without its problems. Nat had picked his singers and dancers—the Merry Young Souls, he called them—for their ability and not their color, consequently he ended up with a thoroughly integrated cast; and, in the early sixties, this worried some people. Las Vegas, for instance, was somewhat dubious about booking the mixed cast in a town that, to say the least, had not exactly been a hotbed of integration. Nevertheless, *Sights and Sounds* went into the Sands Hotel and through five weeks and seventy performances it was a sellout every night. This was even more astounding since it was during the Lenten season, not normally a peak period for show business, and furthermore five other new shows opened in Vegas during that time.

Until then, Harrah's Club in Lake Tahoe, Nevada, where Nat was under a yearly contract to appear, had declined to accept the show. But the Las Vegas success could not be argued; and soon *Sights and Sounds* was drawing capacity crowds to the club's 750-seat Rodeo Room. At the end of its two-week engagement there, it was rebooked for three more weeks in October.

One hotel even offered to double Nat's usual booking

price if he would extend his scheduled tour for an extra week in December to play its main room. But there was one stipulation: the cast would have to be made all-Negro. Nat gave his answer to the show's producer, Ike Jones. "You tell them we'll be happy to meet their demands, provided they'll have all-Negro personnel on their staff when we're playing there."

With his integrated cast, Nat even withdrew his pledge never to play the Deep South again—he had made it nine years before following the attack on him in Birmingham— and performed concerts in Kentucky, Maryland and Tennessee. Again, it was Nat's understanding way of doing what he thought should be done. "I figured that I was important enough in my profession so that if a guy wanted me, he had to take what I brought," Nat said, in explaining why he insisted on using an interracial cast in *Sights and Sounds*. "Sometimes you have to use these weapons. If the big man can't do it how can you expect the little man to do anything? I do a clean show and I have a reputation. I'm not going to bring in anything obscene."

And so, despite the critcism of some of the more narrow-minded militants, my husband fought in his own way with almost his last breath for a better America for black people. I saw him pushing himself, long after some people wondered if he was really in the best of health. One night, as Sparky was strapping the wireless microphone around his waist before showtime, I remarked: "I get the weirdest feeling every-time I see him put that on. He looks like he's about to be executed."

In truth, his days were already numbered.

17

The trouble began in September of 1964, at least as near as anybody around my husband knew at the time. He was playing Lake Tahoe, where I had visited with him briefly before returning home to the children, and commuting to Los Angeles for his role as a strolling balladeer with Stubby Kaye for the musical interludes introducing sequences of the comedy-western *Cat Ballou*. He would finish a show at Harrah's Club at two o'clock in the morning and then a couple of hours later would be catching a plane for Hollywood. There he'd work, nap and catch a plane back for his nightclub act.

Nat began to look worn out and tired and he said so, but he never complained about anything else.

Besides looking and feeling tired, however, he began to lose weight. Nat was lean all his life, and it was natural that with the double activity making him lose a few pounds, he would seem pretty thin. At first, it was just a matter of Sparky punching a new hole in the matching cloth belts Nat wore with his suits. But then, another hole had to be punched, and another. . . .

"You ought to eat something," Sparky told Nat finally, "you're getting too thin."

Nat paid no attention.

Then one day an argument began. "You didn't fix these pants," Nat complained to Sparky as he slipped on a pair of trousers and found them too loose about the waist.

"Nat, I fixed those pants two days ago," Sparky replied, eying him carefully. Then he added, "You ought to see a doctor."

"There ain't nothin' wrong with me but this goddamn picture," Nat snapped irritably. "When I get off of it, I can get my rest. You go see a doctor, because you're the one who's sick."

"No, I'm not sick, but you're gonna make me sick," Sparky retorted, and then he added what was a joke between the two of them, ". . . me with my ulcer."

The argument ended, but the trouble lingered on. A month or so later, after they had moved on to the Sands Hotel in Las Vegas, it flared up in earnest. Nat, like all performers, normally took time to unwind after a show, getting something to eat, having a drink or catching a lounge act. But that Saturday night after his last show, he had gone immediately to his room. "I'm tired. I'm going to bed," he explained.

What Nat didn't reveal was that while he was onstage a drawing, burning pain had stabbed him so hard in the chest that he was barely able to finish singing.

Heading to his hotel suite alone, he had just gotten to the door when the agonizing pain struck again. He pushed the door open and fell to the floor. He crawled to the phone and called for a doctor.

Meanwhile, Sparky, like a good Catholic, was planning to go to 4 A.M. mass and was waiting out the time when his phone rang about 3:30.

By the time Sparky reached Nat's suite, the doctor was already there. Nat would not be able to work for a few days, he declared.

Sparky sat down on the side of the bed and told Nat, "I'd better call your wife."

"No, you don't have to call her," Nat replied.

"What do you mean, I don't have to call her?" Sparky demanded. "When we get home, she's gonna raise hell with me for *not* calling her with you up here sick."

"You don't have to call her," Nat said again.

"Well, I'm gonna call her," Sparky insisted.

"You do and I'll fire you," Nat threatened.

The call did not come, and Nat and his *Sights and Sounds* company moved on to San Francisco for an engagement at a nearby San Carlos theater.

There, the cough and pains continued; and, during a recording session, Nat was difficult and surly, which was totally unlike him. Staying at the Fairmont Hotel, Nat finally had to summon a hotel physician. Of the five doctors who serve the Fairmont, the one who happened to take the call was a prominent physician, who coincidentally had met Nat three years earlier in Florida. He was a gently gracious man, whom I was to have the pleasure of meeting years later. "From the minute I walked into the room," the doctor told me several years later, "I knew he was a very sick man."

The doctor asked my husband when he had last had a physical checkup.

"I just had one in Vegas," Nat told him.

"Did they give you a chest X ray?" the doctor asked.

Nat said they didn't, and the doctor arranged for him to have one at his office. "From the minute we looked at the X rays," the doctor was to tell me later, "we were all broken up. It was obvious that he only had a couple of months."

The doctor immediately put Nat on antibiotics, and advised him to end his engagement there and come home to his own physician.

And still no one told me, not until the eighth day of December. I had just returned from ten days in Europe and planned to stay a day or so at our apartment in New York before flying home. I spoke with my friend Peri Daniels, the wife of singer Billy Daniels, when I arrived, and she suggested that we go see Sammy Davis, Jr., who was performing on Broadway in *Golden Boy* and who was celebrating his birthday that evening.

I was dressed to leave when the telephone rang about 7 P.M., and my sister, Charlotte, was on the line.

"I've been trying to reach you all day," she said. "Nat's here. He's got to go into the hospital. He's been to see the doctor."

"Is it something serious?" I asked.

"Yes, it's serious." Her voice sounded as heavy as her words.

"Let me talk to him," I told Charlotte.

She put him on and I said, as cheerfully as I could, "Hi, honey. I'll be coming home on the next plane."

"All right," came the answer. It was characteristic of Nat to say so little in times when so much needed to be said.

"Okay," I told him. "Let me speak to Charlotte again."

When my sister came back on the line, I told her, "You tell the doctor to call me right this minute."

A few minutes later, the phone rang again. It was the doctor.

I wasted no time. "Doctor, what's wrong with Nat?"

"He's got a tumor on his lung, Maria," he replied.

"Have you X-rayed him?"

"Yes, it's pretty large."

"Is it serious?"

"Well, I think so."

With a sinking sensation, I asked, "Do you think he has cancer of the lung?"

After a moment's hesitation, the answer came, "I think so, Maria. It looks pretty bad."

"I'm catching the next plane."

I hung up the phone—and, in that moment, I knew that my husband was going to die.

18

I was up the remainder of that night—thinking, worrying—
and at five o'clock the next morning some friends drove me
to John F. Kennedy Airport for what was going to be a long
flight to Los Angeles. Dear Glenn Wallichs was waiting for
me when we landed, and he drove me straight to St. John's
Hospital in Santa Monica.

When I walked into Nat's room on the sixth floor, he was
asleep and they had already inserted tubes in his nose and
throat. He looked a little worn.

I later went home to change clothes, then came back and
stayed at the hospital the remainder of the day.

From that time on, I was there every day. The first two
weeks were miserable. Nat was withdrawn and probably a
very frightened man.

It was not until the fourth or fifth day that I saw my husband in actual pain. The back pains came so strong that
Nat could not hide his discomfort. "Oh, my God, I can't
stand this!" he cried out at one point. "Let me die."

My friend Hannah was with me, and we tried moving

him about to ease the pains, but it didn't help. The doctor was not at the hospital at the time, and the staff did not want to give Nat a shot without his permission, although they finally had to. Nat hurt as much or more that day as I ever saw the whole time he was there.

Those first two weeks were perhaps the most trying times for me. Although Nat and I communicated, in a certain sense I just couldn't seem to reach him. It was also during that time that the boxer we had owned for fourteen years, Mr. Pep, had to be put to sleep, and when I told Nat about it, he became upset.

All the time I sat there, during those first days, I knew that my husband was dying, and yet, psychologically, I must have tucked it away in the back of my mind, for nobody had told me there was no chance. When I went to talk with the doctor, he simply reconfirmed his earlier statement that Nat had a lung tumor and he recommended surgery. The doctor was amazed that the complete examination given my husband just six months before, including X rays, had shown no sign of the disease.

It did not take long for Nat's condition to deteriorate. I was standing in the hallway at the hospital one day when he said he would like to come home for Christmas. I went to the doctor, who was standing at the nurses' desk, and asked him if we could do it. "I don't see why not," he replied, and then added, "It might be the last Christmas he'll ever spend at home."

I could see by the faces of some of the people around the desk that they did not appear to think the doctor should have said what he did. But he was simply telling me like it was, and frankly, I wanted to know the truth. I would never have liked to have been fooled, and I don't believe it would have been possible for them to have deluded me about my husband's condition.

As it turned out, however, Nat was in no condition to leave the hospital at Christmas. Instead, the hospital staff let me do something it had never done before, bring all of our children to the hospital to spend the day with their father. The Sisters at St. John's fixed up a room for us and prepared food for all of us. But Nat was so ill he could not help but be a bit irritable, and Casey and Timolin, our three-year-old twins, seemed to be a little frightened of him. We decided not to stay too long, and went back to friends and relatives at home, where it seemed like a wake.

I was living in a kind of daze. I would get up at eight or nine each morning and phone Nat at the hospital. Then I would drive over at noon and stay until eight or ten each night. Only occasionally would I leave for a couple of hours during the middle of the day if there were things that no one else could take care of. But thank God for the wonderful people I had working for me at the time, for they kept our house running. My poor children hardly ever saw me.

Meanwhile, messages of hope and concern poured in from all over the country. Much of it, of course, was from Nat's fellow entertainers, including John Wayne and Arthur Godfrey, both of whom had been lucky enough to battle cancer and win, and from the entire company of the Broadway show *Fiddler on the Roof*. But there were many thousands more. Edmund G. Brown, then Governor of California, sent word, "Get well. I need you." Washington State Senator David G. Cowen wrote, "May God let you sing again for all the world." The Los Angeles County Board of Supervisors and the Police Department of Poughkeepsie, New York, sent their best wishes, as did the Consul General of

Liberia and E. J. (Buzzie) Bavasi, then General Manager of the Los Angeles Dodgers (for whom Nat was the prime backer of their annual all-star night in which Hollywood celebrities appeared, and whose president, Walter O'Malley, refused to allow a memorial benefit for the Nat Cole Cancer Foundation on grounds that he could not throw a benefit for every entertainer who died).

One of the nicest messages of all came from Bob and Ethel Kennedy, in which the Senator declared, "I have decided I will not sing publicly again unless it is with you."

On New Year's, following the bad siege at Christmas, Nat was able to come home for two days. Two nurses were assigned, one for the day and one for the evening, and Nat spent most of the time sitting in our room in his rocking chair. Once he got up and walked out to the playhouse, where Charlotte, some friends and I were sitting on the floor, sorting out some of the thousands of letters that the post office had dropped off by the bags-full. (The postmaster at Santa Monica said it was the most mail ever addressed to one individual in the history of California.) Nat watched us for about five minutes; but he was so weak he could hardly hold his head up. My friends and I tried to act very casual about how he looked; but I think everyone choked up when for a moment his face lit up in wonderment as he remarked: "Is all that for me?" I remember Charlotte (who was his secretary) answering, "Yes, dear. . . . Everyone loves you . . . just like we do."

That night I took him back to the hospital.

Much of the time after that, Nat talked very little. Many people resented the fact that I would not permit them to visit him in the hospital. I willingly bore the brunt of that resentment, but what they did not know was that my husband had told me that he did not want to see them. I could not tell them that, so I just took the blame myself. But Nat was terribly ill then, and didn't feel that he could bear the strain of conversation. There were some exceptions, of course; I usually let him make them. Glenn Wallichs, Jack Benny, Danny Thomas and Frank Sinatra were among them. In his worst days he would smile warmly when a close fellow performer would come to see him.

Naturally, there were some days when Nat felt better than he did on others. When he first entered the hospital, he would sometimes go into the auditorium and play the piano, to the delight of the staff. Once or twice, he even sang a little bit, but he soon gave that up. And he never spoke of the future.

Also, when he was up to it, Nat enjoyed visiting with the nurses in the kitchen, often chastising those whom he saw with cigarettes. He had smoked three packs a day before he was hospitalized; but once there, he never seemed to miss them.

"Oh, Mac, are you smoking?" he said one day to his favorite nurse, Viviane McKenzie. She admitted that she had been addicted to the cigarette habit for thirty years. Nat thought a bit and said, "The thing for us to do is try to keep the young people from starting." He even wanted to go on television to warn American youth of the hazards of smoking; but, of course, he was unable to do so.

(After Nat's death, one of the largest law firms in the East encouraged me to bring a lawsuit against the tobacco industry, blaming their product as the cause, in what would have been a "class suit" on behalf of families of victims of diseases linked to smoking. "With a man the stature of your husband, we firmly believe we could win," I was told.

But in the painful aftermath of his death, I decided not to go through the trying experience of a long court case.)

In addition to all the mail that we handled at home, the hospital was flooded with books, suggested cures, cakes and candies sent to my husband. He was grateful for it all; but the "cures," of course, were worthless, and he had little appetite for much besides ice cream. The nurses would give Nat anything he wanted, and he tried his best to show his gratitude. He presented the sixth-floor workers with a stereo record player at Christmas, and the last photograph taken of my husband was when he posed with some of the nurses and the gift.

As usual with my husband, he ofttimes tried to hide his discomfort even in the hospital. "Don't try to be a martyr," Mac warned him more than once. "If you're having pain, let me know because we've got the wherewithal here to take care of it."

Nat would just laugh softly and reply: "I can't fool you, can I, Mac?"

When one of the women working in the kitchen happened to remark: "I'll never forget Nat King Cole. My husband and I fell in love listening to him sing," Nat heard about it and sent her an autographed picture.

As long as he was able, Nat would go down to the hospital chapel every day, even in a wheelchair. Being a religious man, he seemed to think about everything he had ever done that might have been "wrong"—according to the Christian sense of morality.

"I just want God to forgive me," he would say. Nat never did any more than any normal man; but after Christmas, he became very close to me again, like in the days when we first met, and he told me all the things there were to tell, things that would only come from a man who knew he needed to be close to the one he loved. Yet he never admitted to me that he believed he had reached the end.

One day, with tears streaming down his cheeks, he said weakly, "I'm just so tired, so tired."

"But you have to get well, for me," I told him.

He braced up then and said simply, "Okay."

Another day he was pacing the floor, slapping his fist into an open hand and repeating over and over, "I've got to get well. . . . I've got to get well!"

"Of course you've got to get well," I said casually, "so you can do all the things you still want to do."

"No, no," he answered. "I've got to get well so that I can make you happy!"

All during my husband's illness, we tried to keep a cheerful outlook to the press for the benefit of his public. All of the papers were asking for stories, and we put them off, saying simply, "He's doing as well as can be expected."

When Nat started taking cobalt treatments, for which he had to leave the hospital to go to a special laboratory, it became impossible to avoid the newsmen altogether. One day a reporter and photographer were waiting for us as we came out of the hospital. Nat was obviously very ill and we knew that if pictures of him were printed, they would certainly show it. Nat grayed considerably as his condition worsened, and his weight dropped from 170 to 120 pounds. But the newsmen were very apologetic, and even had tears in their eyes as they pleaded, "Please excuse us, Mr. Cole, but we have orders, and if we don't come back with the pictures, we'll be fired."

Nat agreed to let them shoot, and as we walked away one of them called out, "God bless you."

But the cobalt treatments were unable to halt the spread of cancer, and, on January 25, doctors removed Nat's left lung in a three-hour operation. The word went out that he had responded satisfactorily, and the public, whose prayers and hopes rode on every word of Nat's condition, became overly optimistic, thinking him actually on the road to recovery. There was even a rumor that he might go to Hawaii to further recuperate. What the medical men had actually tried to convey was that my husband's body had agreeably withstood the shock of surgery. Could he sing again, people wanted to know. The medical answer was yes, in that his vocal cords had not been damaged by the disease. But this answer led some to believe that he might soon return to the stage.

All during Nat's hospitalization, his father had been seriously ill in Chicago with a heart ailment. For fear that he could not withstand the shock, Reverend Coles was not told of his son's condition, and several times while in the hospital, Nat had telephoned his father long distance, acting as if he were calling from home. But five days after Nat's operation, his father died. There were great deliberations over whether to tell Nat or not, but since he listened to radio and television constantly, we decided he had to be told. Nat took the terrible news without uttering a word.

Two weeks after the operation, doctors, tracing radioactive isotopes through his body, made a dreadful discovery—the disease had reached Nat's liver. It had been his misfortune to have the virulent and rapid-spreading type of cancer. It was felt from that day my husband could not survive more than a week and a half.

I was in Harold Plant's office when the doctor reached me by phone. "We've just done the liver scan," he said.

"Well?" I asked.

"It's just a matter of days," he replied.

I completely collapsed.

Two days later, on Friday, his condition worsened; and the hospital placed him on the critical list.

Throughout most of that day I was on the telephone, talking with my husband's attorney, Leo Branton, hospital publicist John Kelly, and Ben Irwin, Nat's own publicist. The problem was in trying to prepare the public for the inevitable, since many of his fans expected him to soon be leaving the hospital.

It was decided that a statement should be prepared explaining that Nat's recovery had been slowed somewhat, and that he would have to remain in the hospital longer than had been anticipated. This would have paved the way for further statements of less optimistic nature, and the public could have gradually realized that his condition was terminal.

I was supposed to attend a Baseball Writers' Dinner that very night to receive a trophy in Nat's honor, but now I was certainly in no condition to do so. We asked a good friend, actor Ricardo Montalban, to accept the award in Nat's behalf, and he did. It was a sad evening.

Saturday morning, in one of those inexplicable remissions that sometimes evidences itself in cancer patients, Nat awoke rather cheerful and feeling better. He even sat up on the side of the bed to have breakfast. We quickly moved to stop any announcement going out concerning his health. Nat, almost always, had the television set on in his room, and there was a great fear that he would hear some newscast saying that his condition was failing.

In a rare stroke of good timing, that very day some newspapers carried an interview with my husband—the questions had been submitted in writing to me—in which there was every indication that he fully expected to recover.

Sunday was Valentine's Day, and the weather was beautiful. Nat was feeling well enough to want to go for a ride down by the beach, so we put him in the car, oxygen equipment and all. Charlotte drove, and we carried Nat's nurse, Mac, with us as well as a dear friend from Chicago, Dr. Scott.

We were gone for nearly an hour and a half.

When we got back, some members of the hospital staff were waiting outside with a wheelchair. "Let us help you, Nat," one of them offered.

"No, thank you," Nat said, getting out slowly and walking. "I can help myself."

All of us stood with our hearts in our mouths, hoping he wouldn't fall.

Charlotte parked the car while the rest of us went upstairs. Nat, having finally accepted the wheelchair, waited by a window in the hallway outside his room, while the nurse and I went inside to straighten things up a bit.

As Nat sat there, looking out at the California mountains turning purple in the last light of day, Charlotte came up behind him and put her arm around his shoulders. He reached back and took her hand in his and squeezed it gently.

"Turn me away," he said.

19

K. C. (Casey) Bower arrived at St. John's Hospital during
the fading hours of Sunday evening to begin her regular 11
P.M. to 7 A.M. shift.

The man she had cared for all these weeks had never
really been a stranger to her. The past summer she had
gone on crutches with her left leg in a cast (due to surgery
for a dislocated toe) to the Hollywood Bowl to hear Nat in
concert, and had become so enthralled with the music that
she had hardly been able to fall asleep when she returned
home. Furthermore, during his days in the hospital, she
had discovered in one of those strange little twists that fate
seems to love an almost certain link between herself and
Nat's first days with the trio.

A Canadian by birth, Casey had been a nurse since she
first came to California in 1934. About 1939, her cousin
came to visit her in Los Angeles, and a patient whom Casey
had been caring for over the years was kind enough to send
them out on the town for an evening. Among the places
they dropped into was a little bar on La Brea, where a trio

was performing with a slender young black man playing
piano and singing. Casey's cousin flipped. "I think he is the
greatest!" she told Casey.

Casey liked him too, but it was a few years yet before
Nat King Cole became a star, and Casey thought no more
about the group she had seen in the Hollywood club. It was
only after she came to the hospital to care for Nat, and she
had listened to him recount his early days at the Swanee
Inn, that she realized he was the one she had taken her
cousin to see.

Maybe all of this was why Casey had felt such complete
familiarity with Nat from the beginning of her time with him
at the hospital. She had heard that he was ill; but she, a
private-duty nurse, had not expected the call that came from
the Supervisor of Nurses at St. John's, telling her, "I want
you to take care of Nat King Cole."

When she reported for duty on December 12, four days
after my husband entered the hospital, she found a bright
and cheerful patient. He was sitting in a mahogany rocking
chair upholstered in antique blue velvet, which I had given
him for Christmas the year before, and reading the Bible.
Casey was introduced to "Mr. Cole."

"You've always been Nat King Cole to me," Casey said
quickly, "so I'll call you Nat, if you don't mind."

"That's great," he told her. "I'll call you Casey."

And that's the way it was.

Casey soon changed one impression she had formed of
Nat. She had decided, when she first saw him with the Bible
in his hand, that here was another ill person trying to quickly
catch up on his spiritual shortcomings. But she later discovered the Bible showed the kind of wear incurred by long and
frequent usage, and that Nat could quickly turn to almost

any section or passage in it. Many nights, when she came on duty, she found him sitting in the rocker, reading the Bible.

Casey spent New Year's with Nat, me and the children at home and remembers vividly how important it was to him to be able to leave the hospital at that time. It was almost as if he had known it might be his last visit. Nat surprised Casey that New Year's evening when, as he sat with his back to the piano, Sweetie sat down to play. Casey did not detect anything out of the ordinary in her playing until Nat, without looking around, said to Sweetie, "Why don't you use both hands, dear?"

At the hospital, Nat and Casey often walked the halls, causing a minor commotion wherever they went. Nurses, doctors and patients all flocked to Nat, and those who were bedridden would call to him as he passed by if their doors were open. Nat's own door often had to be closed and locked to keep out strangers who had managed to find out his room number and who would often climb six flights of back stairs and enter through the fire exit, which was next to it. The nurses rigged up a bell that would ring whenever that stairway door was opened, and it was their signal that an unauthorized person was in the vicinity.

When they walked the halls, Casey would often slip her arm through Nat's. Not to help him in anyway, for he did not like to be helped, but because he was her patient and it was her prerogative: She could walk with her arm in his if she wanted to.

Casey often sang to Nat at night. It had started with what she considered to be almost a joke. She had been rubbing his back and listening to a song on television she liked, and had, rather absentmindedly, begun to sing along with it. Suddenly, she stopped short and gasped, "Oh, gosh! Imagine me, singing before the master!"

"Please don't stop, Casey," Nat told her. "Go on and sing."

So she began to sing anytime something came on that she knew the words to.

Casey was the last person to hear my husband sing. It happened one night in the room while they were watching Kate Smith on the Tonight show. Suddenly, Nat burst into song with Kate, and when they both had finished, Nat declared that Kate got better every year. He could hardly contain himself because of the pure joy of listening, and when she sang again, Nat sang again too. Later, Casey could not remember what the two songs were, but yet, strangely enough, she knows she'll never forget them.

As she came on duty that Sunday night, she noticed the drastic change in Nat's condition. Although he had gotten around fairly well on Saturday, even going for a visit in the nurses' quarters, this night he was much weaker, and asked Casey to help him get about. Though weak and thin, he was still so tall that he had to lean down on her shoulders and he was apologetic because he felt that he was so heavy upon her. Yet he wanted to walk to prove to himself that he could. Then he would have spells of weakness when he got back to his bed and would put his head down, then rise up quickly, trying to fight it off.

"Casey, what's the matter with me?" he would ask, over and over again, sitting up straight.

Casey had been concerned about Nat ever since his surgery, for she had noticed the change in his condition then. Before he had seemed anxious to get back to work, now he never mentioned it.

Sunday night, Casey was worried, but she wanted to calm Nat so when he asked her about his weakness, she explained it away casually. "You've had some medicine," she told him, "and I've had that same medicine once or twice. It makes you feel terrible. You don't know where you are or what you're doing half the time. I know from experience, and you're probably having the same reaction that I had."

Casey even tried to take Nat's mind off his increasing weakness. She told him about her Schnauzer dog which was going to deliver two puppies by Caesarean birth. "What are you going to name them?" Nat asked.

"Oh, I think I'll probably call one of them Nathaniel," she said slyly. "What do you think I ought to name the other one?"

Nat thought for a moment. "Name him Chauncey," he said finally.

"Okay," Casey agreed.

Casey kept the lights soft in the room through the night, and, as they made trip after trip over to the rocking chair and back to the bed that was slightly raised on one side, she would hold his hand in such a way that he could not really tell that she was quietly checking the strength of his pulse. She would sit down on the low side of the bed and help support him, and pat his hand while keeping one finger on the inside of his wrist. She took his temperature only at the scheduled intervals, for again, she did not wish to alarm him.

Nat did not complain of pain that evening, and required no medication from Casey. Yet she felt he was suffering, and compassion welled up inside her.

Conversation between the two of them had now almost ceased, except his occasional queries about his growing weakness, and Casey again explained about the drugs.

"Oh, you think it might be this medicine?" Nat would ask for reassurance.

"Well, I'm pretty sure of it," she told him.

Casey thought of calling the doctor or me, but she knew that to call from the phone in the room, or if she suddenly disappeared to telephone from outside, would only alarm Nat further.

Besides, there was nothing anyone could do.

Nat lay back on the bed once more and began to repeat a name. Because of the lateness of her duty shift, Casey had spent little time with Nat and me together, thus, the name meant nothing to her. Nat said it several times. The name was "Skeez."

Although the weakness had almost completely overcome him, Nat's voice, naturally soft, was nevertheless positive.

Realizing that Nat was still alert and lucid, Casey questioned him, "Who do you mean, Nat? I don't know anybody by that name."

"Maria," Nat said. He did not speak again.

He raised up, then lay back once more. Casey spoke to him, and then, believing he no longer understood her, she went to the phone and called the doctor. "I think you had better get over right now."

Casey went back to Nat. He was lying on his back, but turned slightly on his right side, with his head facing the door.

He drifted away.

It was 5:30 in the morning.

20

There is little that I remember about the next four days, except that the weather was beautiful. I moved about in a mental and emotional haze, touching reality only in occasional moments.

Driving home from the mortuary, after making funeral arrangements that first day, I recall suddenly seeing, at my neighborhood newsstand, the glaring headline: "NAT KING COLE DEAD OF CANCER." To this day when I pass that newsstand, with the same little man standing there, I still see that headline.

Sweetie flew in from the school she was attending in the East, and friends met her at the airport. Henry Miller's wife, Jane, a dear friend through the years, took her to shop for something to wear. Jim Conkling helped me pick out a suit for Nat to be buried in. Smitty, Nat's barber of many years, cut his hair, and Sparky dressed him, finding that his identification bracelet was on the wrong hand. I left his original wedding band on his finger.

At the new Los Angeles Music Center, of which Nat was a founder-member and where he was to have performed at its opening eight weeks earlier, flags were flown at half-mast, as they were at the Musicians' Union local on Vine Street. At City Hall, the fifteen-man City Council adjourned in mourning. That Monday night in a St. Louis club, Ike Cole sang a medley of his brother's songs before dissolving into tears.

The telegrams, cards and notes of condolences came in an endless stream.

One of the most touching moments came when a guard, who drove one of the cars that patrolled our home, came into the house while people were calling on me to pay their respects. I came downstairs to greet him, and he fell to his knees, saying, "Oh, Mrs. Cole, I'm so sorry. I'm not worthy, but can my son and I come in our uniforms to the funeral?"

I was overwhelmed with tears as I reached out to touch him and tell him that they were very welcome.

On Wednesday, the sealed, coffee-colored coffin was taken to St. James' Episcopal Church on Wilshire Boulevard, and for seven hours thousands of people—some who knew my husband, others who knew him not at all except through his music—filed quietly through the church. Some showed no sign of emotion, others wept openly, as did one elderly woman who sat near the coffin, her tears spilling down over one of Nat's albums that she clutched to her bosom.

Some of the people bore the look of wealth; others were obviously poor. They were all colors and ages; and they all shared a common emotion: sorrow.

The next day was as beautiful as the three that had preceded it, even though the temperature rose to 80 degrees by noon. It was the day of the funeral.

The pallbearers assembled at the house early, Jim Conkling, Lee Gillette, Marvin Fisher, Jack Leonard, Harold Plant, John Collins, Glenn Wallichs, Sam Weiss, Dave

Cavanaugh, Carlos Gastel and Henry Miller were the men who would bear Nat on his last journey. As the hour of the funeral neared, Marvin Fisher, the song publisher who had been my husband's friend and business associate for two decades, turned to the others and said, "He's been carrying us all our lives; now it's our turn to carry him."

Although only 400 persons were permitted inside St. James' for the services, another 3,000 had gathered outside, where two dozen policemen were assembled to direct traffic and keep order. The crowd gave them no problem; there was no hysteria, no commotion. When one woman collapsed in the heat, another quietly slipped under the restraining ropes and went to a policeman to tell him. She did not call out.

The crowd remained subdued even when the long black limousines began arriving with the honorary pallbearers shortly before 11 A.M. Quietly, they watched them enter: Jack Benny, George Burns, Johnny Mathis, Billy Daniels, Sammy Davis, Jr., Eddie (Rochester) Anderson, Ricardo Montalban, Danny Thomas, Gordon Jenkins, Nelson Riddle, Ralph Carmichael, Frank Sinatra, Peter Lawford, Billy May, Pat Kennedy Lawford, Stan Kenton, Jimmy Durante, Jimmy McHugh, Dr. David Daniels, Steve Allen, Jack Entratter, Ivan Mogull, Sammy Cahn, Milton Berle, Jimmy Van Heusen, Dr. James Scott, Charlie Harris, George Jessel, Frankie Laine, Governor Edmund G. Brown, Alan Livingston, Bobby Darin, Jerry Lewis, and one other who has since joined Nat in death: Sy Devore, Nat's tailor.

Among the great and near-great who came to pay their respects was another whose own tragic death was less than seven months away: actress Dorothy Dandridge, who was the godmother of our twin girls.

The services, which included a High Mass, lasted an

hour and fifteen minutes, during which both Jack Benny
and George Jessel joined in the final tribute. "I refuse to believe," George said, "that The Great Creator, who made
roses bloom . . . would let anything die. . . . Sweet dreams,
good man." And Jack Benny, remembering some of the
songs that Nat had given to millions, consoled us all as he
said, "Time, as always, will work its healing ways, and I
know that someday the dewdrops will glisten on the 'Rambling Rose'; the 'Ballerina' will dance again, and 'Mona
Lisa' will smile."

As difficult as that moment was for all of us, I feel it may
have been hardest for my young son, Kelly. Cookie was
twenty and Sweetie fifteen, certainly old enough to understand what it was all about. Casey and Timolin were but
three years old, too young to really know. But Kelly had
turned six but a week before, and was terribly frightened by
it all. I may have made a great mistake taking him to the
funeral. He was so tiny and so sensitive, and maybe, having
never known his real father and then having lost a second
one who loved him very much, he was wondering at that
moment what would become of him. When he's older,
maybe he'll be able to explain how he felt; maybe he'll say
that had I not taken him he would have felt left out, that
he wanted very much to go to his father's funeral. I did
what I thought I should do at the time. Once, during the
services, Kelly turned to me and said, "Let me just touch the
casket." Later, that magnificent little boy sat with me in
the mausoleum at Forest Lawn and shook everyone's hand.

My husband was laid to rest in a crypt alongside other
great stars.

One of the most beautiful and heart-rending tributes paid
to Nat appeared in *Daily Variety* (a trade publication) that

morning. It was a personal statement from the Chairman of the Board of Capitol Records, our friend Glenn Wallichs. In it, he said:

"Nat Cole is gone and I know that I should find solace in the recordings that remain. But I cannot. His records convey the wonderful voice but not the wonderful man. I thank God I knew him long and well, and in his memory I find reassurance for the future of all our lives.

"Nat Cole's fame rested not on hit records or onstage performances, but on his conduct as a human being. Certainly he set a magnificent example for his own race; but even more, he set an example for all races. He won the admiration of people throughout the world with his unique voice, his matchless demeanor, his natural grace. We must lament his sudden departure from life, but we must also revel in how well that life was lived.

"It is comforting to know that the human race is still capable of producing a Nat Cole. We must be grateful for the lessons he taught: lessons of love, tolerance, work, art, dedication. It is a cliché to suggest that 'we are better men for having known him.' But in Nat's case the clichés are fitting and true: great artist, musician's musician, nice guy. No artist has ever meant so much to me before; none can ever mean so much again.

"I pray that Nat has found eternal rest, secure in the love of his fellow men."

Perhaps Nat has indeed found eternal rest. But I remember something he said once when we were discussing the theory of reincarnation. "If I am ever reincarnated," he said, "I want to come back as my wife—nobody else ever had it so good."

He was right, you know.

EPILOGUE

More than half a decade has passed since the death of my husband, and I have attempted here to do but one thing: to let those who were his admirers know more about Nat Cole the father, the husband, the man. If I had chosen another title for these collected memories, it could only have been A *Gentle Man*.

For a while, after Nat's death, I returned to the stage and put together an act that debuted in Australia in the winter of 1966. I tried singing again out of a need to keep busy. I've always been the type of woman who had to have something to do; not necessarily show business, but something I could relate to and that I could give a lot to, from whatever resources that are within me. For part of 1967, show business was it, and I felt alive once more. But because of the time I would have needed to spend in small clubs around the country to perfect an act that would have been acceptable in the industry, I decided, after a few engagements, to "call it quits" rather than appear in places that would have, in the public's eye, diminished the image of Mrs. Nat Cole.

However, I had the opportunity later to co-host a local television show on Los Angeles Station KHJ. The show was a daily stint divided into three hour-long segments, and during my portion of it, over a period of time, I interviewed everybody from black militants to the Vice President of the United States. Before it was over, I had received hate letters, threats on my life, and a great deal of praiseworthy fan mail.

It was constructive, challenging and interesting and, even though I left the job of my own accord, I sincerely feel it was the making of Maria Cole, the individual.

One major network expressed interest in my working for them, but frankly there are still problems with what to do with black women in the industry on network TV. I have had visions of doing further work in the industry, but only time will tell.

As far as singing goes, I would never want to sing again seriously, except maybe in the bathtub.

A good deal of my time during the first two years has been spent in establishing, with the help of some wonderful people, the Nat King Cole Cancer Foundation as a memorial to my late husband.

Nat's friends and fans raised $50,000 to establish a room in the Wilson Pavilion of the UCLA Medical Center. There is a plaque on the door that reads: "Donated by the Nat King Cole Cancer Foundation."

Some of the doctors I met there were very gracious, namely Dr. Donald Rochlin and Dr. Sherman Mellinkoff, who was dean of the Medical School. Strangely enough, also, the afternoon I was invited to visit, I met members of the Wilson family, who could not have been more gracious or appreciative. The chancellor of the university, however, barely acknowledged me when I was introduced to him. Maybe he didn't catch the name.

Why, then, did we choose UCLA in the first place? Because of the interest that both my late husband and I had in the UCLA Elementary School, which our son, Kelly, attended. At that time it was headed by Dr. John Goodlad and Dr. Madeline Hunter, two of the finest educators I have ever met.

I have just agreed to donate to the University of Southern

California all of my husband's memorabilia; this will include all his trophies, plaques, dozens of scrapbooks, gold records, and maybe even his checkered hats. How fortunate it is that my sister Charlotte insisted upon preserving almost everything that pertained to his career and our personal lives.

In the strange and tinsel town in which I live, with the passing of a great man, the lives of his family ofttimes take on a rather diminished and mundane existence. But how marvelous it is for me to be able to say that the really close friends we had in the industry my husband loved so much have remained close to me and my children: the Edward G. Robinsons, the Danny Thomases, the Abe Lipseys, the Billy Danielses, the Paul Burkes, the Jean Louises, the Glenn Wallichs, and so many others.

Nat Cole, of course, is still alive through his music, and, I pray, he forever will be. Through the loud and frequently disagreeable onslaught of rock 'n' roll, his kind of song has lasted, to be returned to us by today's youth (think of "Mona Lisa" and "Nature Boy"). Nat's own popularity, which remained among the top ten performers on the Capitol Records label for years after his death, will return—not as a bit of camp fad, but for the full, rich sweetness of eternity. (It is little wonder that some of his greatest popularity is abroad, where in some years the royalties from his records have exceeded domestic earnings. On our trips to South America, welcoming crowds of over 10,000 people stormed airports to meet his plane.

Someone once told me, and I quote: "Maria, happiness does not always come in the form other people think it should." My oldest daughter, Carol, has said to me innumerable times, "Love is all." Maybe that is stretching it a bit, but it seemed to work for Nat and his legion of fans. Believe me, it worked with his family.

Maria Cole
1971

DISCOGRAPHY OF NAT KING COLE

on Capitol, Starline, Music for Pleasure, and World Record Club Records available August 1972

Title	Recording Date	Single/ EP Nos.	Album Nos.
Straighten Up and Fly Right	30 Nov 43		
Gee, Baby, Ain't I Good to You?	30 Nov 43		
Jumpin' at Capitol	30 Nov 43		
If You Can't Smile Say Yes Please	30 Nov 43		
Sweet Lorraine	15 Dec 43		
Embraceable You	15 Dec 43		
It's Only a Paper Moon	15 Dec 43		
I Can't See for Lookin'	15 Dec 43		
The Man I Love	17 Jan 44		
Body and Soul	17 Jan 44		
Prelude in C Sharp Minor	17 Jan 44		
What Is This Thing Called Love?	17 Jan 44		
After You Get What You Want	6 Mar 44		
Look What You've Done to Me	6 Mar 44		
Easy Listenin' Blues	6 Mar 44		
I Realize Now	6 Mar 44		
There I've Said It Again	28 Nov 44		
Please Consider Me	28 Nov 44		
Bring Another Drink	28 Nov 44		
You Can Depend on Me	30 Mar 45		
If I Could Be With You	30 Mar 45		
Stormy Weather	30 Mar 45		
Riffamarole	30 Mar 45		
I Love to Make Love to You	13 Apr 45		
I'm a Shy Guy	13 Apr 45		
Katusha	13 Apr 45		
You're Nobody 'Til Somebody Loves You	19 May 45		
Don't Blame Me	19 May 45		
I'm Thru with Love	19 May 45		
Barcarolle	23 May 45		
Sweet Georgia Brown	23 May 45		
I Thought You Ought to Know	23 May 45		
It Only Happens Once (remake of master 615)	23 May 45		

Flagalapa	2 Aug 45
It's Better to Be By Yourself (remake of master 751)	11 Oct 45
Come to Baby Do	11 Oct 45
The Frim Fram Sauce	11 Oct 45
I'm an Errand Boy for Rhythm	18 Oct 45
This Way Out	18 Oct 45
I Know That You Know	18 Oct 45
How Does It Feel?	4 Dec 45
You Must Be Blind	4 Dec 45
Loan Me Two Till Tuesday	4 Dec 45
I'm in the Mood for Love (remake of master 644)	15 Mar 46
I Don't Know Why	15 Mar 46
Get Your Kicks on Route 66	15 Mar 46
Everyone Is Saying Hello Again	15 Mar 46
What Can I Say, Dear, After I Say I'm Sorry?	5 Apr 46
To a Wild Rose	5 Apr 46
Baby All the Time (remake of master 1071)	17 Apr 46
Could 'Ya	17 Apr 46
Oh But I Do	17 Apr 46
Rhumba à la King	17 Apr 46
She's My Buddy's Chick (remake of master 840)	1 May 46
You Call It Madness But I Call It Love	1 May 46
Homeward Bound	1 May 46
Chant of the Blues	1 May 46
The Christmas Song (remake of master 956)	19 Aug 46
The Best Man	19 Aug 46
You Should Have Told Me (remake of master 957)	19 Aug 46
(I Love You) for Sentimental Reasons	22 Aug 46
In the Cool of the Evening	6 Sep 46
That's the Beginning of the End	6 Sep 46
If You Don't Like My Apples	17 Sep 46

Poor Butterfly	13 Aug 47	
How High the Moon	13 Aug 47	
I'll Never Be the Same	13 Aug 47	
These Foolish Things	13 Aug 47	
Cole Capers	13 Aug 47	
Three Little Words	13 Aug 47	
Blues in My Shower	13 Aug 47	
I Wanna Be a Friend of Yours	15 Aug 47	
Three Blind Mice	15 Aug 47	
We'll Save the Bones for Henry Jones	20 Aug 47	MFP 1432
My Baby Likes to Be-Bop	20 Aug 47	
Harmony	20 Aug 47	
You Can't Make Money Dreamin'	20 Aug 47	
Wiegenlied	22 Aug 47	
Nature Boy	22 Aug 47	
Wildroot Charlie	22 Aug 47	
Laguna Mood	27 Aug 47	
I'm a Little Ashamed	28 Aug 47	
Now He Tells Me (remake)	28 Aug 47	
That's a Natural Fact	28 Aug 47	
Lament in Chords	29 Aug 47	
You've Got Another Heart on Your Hands	29 Aug 47	
Baby I Need You	29 Aug 47	
Those Things Money Can't Buy	29 Aug 47	
The Love Nest	28 Oct 47	
Dream a Little Dream of Me	28 Oct 47	
Then I'll Be Tired of You	28 Oct 47	
I Feel So Smoochie	4 Nov 47	
The Boy from Texas (The Girl from Tennessee)	4 Nov 47	
When You Walked Out with Shoes On	4 Nov 47	
That's the Kind of Girl I Dream Of	4 Nov 47	
The Geek	6 Nov 47	
Confess	6 Nov 47	
If I Had You	6 Nov 47	
Money Is Honey	3 Nov 47	
Little Girl	3 Nov 47	
Who's Telling You Lies?	3 Nov 47	

No Moon At All	3 Nov 47	
It's the Sentimental Thing to Do	5 Nov 47	
I've Only Myself to Blame	5 Nov 47	
It's Like Taking Candy From a Baby	5 Nov 47	
You've Changed	5 Nov 47	
Flo and Joe	7 Nov 47	
If You Stub Your Toe on the Moon	7 Nov 47	
I'm Gonna Spank My Heart	7 Nov 47	
I See By the Papers	7 Nov 47	
Return Trip	7 Nov 47	
A Woman Always Understands	7 Nov 47	
Put 'Em in a Box	24 Nov 47	
Blue and Sentimental	24 Nov 47	
I've Got a Way with Women	24 Nov 47	
My Fair Lady	24 Nov 47	
I Wish I Had the Blues Again	29 Nov 47	
Didn't I Tell You So?	29 Nov 47	
Lost April	20 Dec 47	
Lillette	20 Dec 47	
Monday Again	20 Dec 47	
Lulu Belle	20 Dec 47	
It's So Hard to Laugh (It's So Easy to Cry)	20 Dec 47	
Portrait of Jenny	14 Jan 49	ST 21139/SRS 5039
Vesti La Guibba (Laugh Cool Clown)	22 Mar 49	
Bop-Kick	22 Mar 49	
For All We Know	22 Mar 49	
Land of Love	29 Mar 49	
Lush Life	29 Mar 49	MFP 1049
Lillian	29 Mar 49	
'Tis Autumn	29 Mar 49	
Yes Sir, That's My Baby	29 Mar 49	
I Used to Love You	30 Mar 49	
Etymology (The Language of Love)	30 Mar 49	
Peaches	30 Mar 49	
Last But Not Least	30 Mar 49	
I Wake Up Screaming, Dreaming of You	30 Mar 49	

It Was So Good While It Lasted	20 May 49	
Roses and Wine	20 May 49	
Who Do You Know in Heaven?	20 May 49	
I Get Sentimental Over Nothing	20 May 49	
A Little Yellow Ribbon	20 May 49	
Your Voice	20 May 49	
Two Front Teeth	2 Aug 49	
You Can't Lose a Broken Heart	2 Aug 49	
Bang Bang Boogie	2 Aug 49	
Here Is My Heart	9 Sep 49	
The Horse Told Me	9 Sep 49	
Don't Shove, I'm Leaving	9 Sep 49	
Calypso Blues	9 Sep 49	
Mule Train	7 Nov 49	
My Baby Just Cares for Me	7 Nov 49	
Baby, Won't You Say You Love Me?	9 Feb 50	
I Almost Lost My Mind	9 Feb 50	
A Little Bit Independent	9 Feb 50	
Twister Stockins	9 Feb 50	
I'll Never Say "Never Again" Again	9 Feb 50	MFP 1049
For You, My Love	5 Jan 50	
Can I Come in for a Second?	5 Jan 50	
Always You	11 Mar 50	
The Magic Tree	11 Mar 50	
Mona Lisa	11 Mar 50	
The Greatest Inventor of Them All	11 Mar 50	
Who's Who	11 Mar 50	
Make Believe Land	25 Aug 50	
Get to Gettin'	25 Aug 50	
Frosty, the Snow Man	25 Aug 50	MFP 5224
Little Christmas Tree	25 Aug 50	MFP 5224
Song of Delilah	25 Aug 50	MFP 1049/SM 136
Orange Colored Sky	16 Aug 50	
Jam-bo	16 Aug 50	
My Mother Told Me		
Exactly Like You		SM 136
Jet	13 Dec 50	
Paint Yourself a Rainbow	13 Dec 50	
Destination Moon	13 Dec 50	

I Wish I Were Somebody Else	12 Feb 51	
You Can't Make Me Love You	12 Feb 51	
Red Sails in the Sunset	12 Feb 51	ST 21687/SM 135
I'll Always Remember You	12 Feb 51	
Poor Jenny Is A-Weeping	12 Feb 51	
That's My Gal	1 Feb 51	
Early American	6 Feb 51	
Too Young	6 Feb 51	
Because of Rain	6 Feb 51	
The Day Isn't Long Enough	9 Mar 51	
Little Child	9 Mar 51	SM 136
A Robin and a Rainbow and a Red Red Rose	9 Mar 51	
Lighthouse in the Sky	9 Mar 51	
Pigtails and Freckles	9 Mar 51	
Unforgettable	17 Aug 51	
My First and My Last Love	17 Aug 51	
Lovelight	17 Aug 51	
Walkin' My Baby Back Home	4 Sep 51	
What Does It Take to Make You, etc.	4 Sep 51	
Walkin'	4 Sep 51	
I'm Hurtin'	4 Sep 51	
I Still See Elisa	14 Sep 51	
Miss Me	14 Sep 51	ST 2820
Weaver of Dreams	14 Sep 51	MFP 1049
Wine, Women and Song	14 Sep 51	
Here's to My Lady	14 Sep 51	ST 2820/MFP 1049/ SM 135
It's OK for TV	14 Sep 51	
The Ruby and the Pearl	14 Sep 51	SM 132
The Story of My Wife	14 Sep 51	
You Will Never Grow Old	10 Jan 52	
Easter Sunday	10 Jan 52	
You Weren't There	10 Jan 52	
Somewhere Along the Way	10 Jan 52	
It's Crazy	11 Jan 52	
Where Were You?	11 Jan 52	
You Stepped Out of a Dream	11 Jan 52	SRS 5039/SM 133

Summer Is a Comin' In	11 Jan 52	
Funny (Not Much)	11 Jan 52	
Rough Ridin'	31 Mar 52	
Can't I? (remade on master 2879)	31 Mar 52	
Penthouse Serenade	31 Mar 52	
Rose Room	31 Mar 52	
Polka Dots and Moonbeams	31 Mar 52	
Somebody Loves Me	31 Mar 52	
Melody in F	31 Mar 52	
If I Should Lose You	31 Mar 52	
By the Old Mill Stream	31 Mar 52	
Laura	31 Mar 52	
Don't Let Your Eyes Go Shopping for Your Heart	24 Jul 52	
Strange	28 Jul 52	
How Do I Go About It?	28 Jul 52	
Sweet William	31 Jul 52	
Because You're Mine	31 Jul 52	ST 21689/SM 135
Sleeping Beauty	31 Jul 52	
I'm Never Satisfied	31 Jul 52	
Flaming Heart	12 Aug 52	
Faith Can Move Mountains	12 Aug 52	
Too Soon	12 Aug 52	
Small Towns Are Smile Towns	12 Aug 52	
Mother Nature and Father Time	30 Dec 52	
When I'm Alone	30 Dec 52	
Pretend	30 Dec 52	
A Fool Was I	30 Dec 52	ST 2820
Angel Eyes	14 Jan 53	
Lover Come Back to Me	14 Jan 53	SRS 5039
Can't I	14 Jan 53	
The Magic Window	20 Jan 53	
That's All	20 Jan 53	
Annabelle	20 Jan 53	
If Love Is Good to Me	20 Jan 53	
Blue Gardenia	20 Jan 53	
Dinner for One Please, James	27 Jan 53	
There Goes My Heart	27 Jan 53	SRS 5039
A Handful of Stars	27 Jan 53	

Love Is Here to Stay	27 Jan 53	
A Little Street Where Old Friends Meet	27 Jan 53	
Tenderly	27 Jan 53	SM 136
Almost Like Being in Love	28 Jan 53	SRS 5039
This Can't Be Love	28 Jan 53	
Don't Hurt That Girl	28 Jan 53	
Return to Paradise	31 Mar 53	
Make Her Mine	31 Mar 53	
Why Can't We Try Again?	31 Mar 53	
I Am in Love	31 Mar 53	
Why?	24 Aug 53	
Darling, Je Vous Aime Beaucoup	24 Aug 53	
Little Fingers	24 Aug 53	
I Envy	24 Aug 53	
For a Moment of Your Love	24 Aug 53	
Sleeping Beauty	24 Aug 53	
The Christmas Song (remake of 172)	24 Aug 53	MFP 5224
The Little Boy That Santa Claus Forgot	18 Aug 53	MFP 5224
You're Wrong, All Wrong	18 Aug 53	
Mrs. Santa Claus	18 Aug 53	MFP 5224
Answer Me My Love	3 Dec 53	
Ain't She Sweet?	3 Feb 54	
What to Do	3 Feb 54	
Alone Too Long	9 Feb 54	SM 134
It Happens to Be Me	9 Feb 54	
Unbelievable	9 Feb 54	
Marilyn	9 Feb 54	
Haggi Baba	27 Jul 54	
Smile	27 Jul 54	
I'll Always Be Remembering	24 Aug 54	ST 2820
My One Sin	24 Aug 54	SRS 5039
I'll Never Settle for Less	24 Aug 54	
United	24 Aug 54	
Open Up the Doghouse	7 Sep 54	MFP 1432
Long Long Ago	7 Sep 54	MFP 1432
If I Give My Heart to You	18 Oct 54	SM 135
Hold My Hand	18 Oct 54	
Papa Loves Mambo	18 Oct 54	
Teach Me Tonite	18 Oct 54	

The Sand and the Sea	20 Dec 54	
A Blossom Fell	20 Dec 54	
Forgive My Heart	20 Dec 54	
I'm Gonna Laugh You Right Out of My Life	20 Dec 54	
If I May	20 Dec 54	
I'd Rather Have the Blues	25 Mar 55	
I Hear Music	7 Jun 55	
My Heart Stood Still	7 Jun 55	
I Never Knew	7 Jun 55	
Tea for Two	7 Jun 55	
Nothing Ever Changes	7 Jun 55	
Breezin' Along with the Breeze	7 Jun 55	
Someone You Love	9 Jun 55	
Unfair	9 Jun 55	
Wishing Well	10 Jun 55	ST 2759
I've Learned	10 Jun 55	
Half a Mind	10 Jun 55	
But Not for Me	10 Jun 55	
What Can I Say After I Say I'm Sorry	11 Jun 55	SM 134
It Was That Kiss	11 Jun 55	
Taking a Chance on Love	11 Jun 55	
Don't Blame Me	14 Jul 55	
It Can Happen to You	14 Jul 55	
I Surrender, Dear	14 Jul 55	
Little Girl	14 Jul 55	
Autumn Leaves	23 Aug 55	SRS 5039/ST 2168
Let's Fall In Love	25 Aug 55	SM 131
There Will Never Be Another You	25 Aug 55	SM 131
Just One of Those Things	27 Aug 55	
I Want to Be Happy	27 Aug 55	
You Are My Sunshine	27 Aug 55	
Up Pops Love	27 Aug 55	
Love Me as Though There Were No Tomorrow	20 Dec 55	
Too Young to Go Steady	20 Dec 55	
Dreams Can Tell a Lie	20 Dec 55	
Back in My Arms	20 Dec 55	ST 2820
Dame Crazy	29 Dec 55	
I Just Found Out About Love	29 Dec 55	SM 133
My Personal Possession	29 Dec 55	
That's All There Is to That	29 Dec 55	

Mr. Juke Box	29 Dec 55	
I Got Love	29 Dec 55	
Stay	29 Dec 55	
Believe	29 Dec 55	
Night Lights	4 Jan 56	
To the Ends of the Earth	4 Jan 56	
Never Let Me Go	4 Jan 56	SM 132
The Shadows	4 Jan 56	
I Promise You	4 Jan 56	SM 136
The Way I Love You	4 Jan 56	
Once Before	21 Jan 56	
I'm Willing to Share This with You	21 Jan 56	
I Need a Plan	21 Jan 56	
The Story's Old	21 Jan 56	
Unfair	21 Jan 56	ST 2759
Make Me	21 Jan 56	
Sometimes I Wonder	21 Jan 56	
We Are Americans Too	17 May 56	
You Can Depend on Me	15 Aug 56	
Candy	15 Aug 56	
Sweet Lorraine	15 Aug 56	SM 133
It's Only a Paper Moon	15 Aug 56	
Get Your Kicks On Route 66	15 Aug 56	SM 132
Don't Let it Go to Your Head	14 Sep 56	
You're Lookin' at Me	14 Sep 56	SM 135
I Was a Little Too Lonely	14 Sep 56	
Just You Just Me	14 Sep 56	SM 132
How Little We Know	19 Sep 56	
Ballerina	19 Sep 56	ST 2434/SW3-1613/ SW 20664
Should I?	19 Sep 56	
Caravan	21 Sep 56	
Lonely One	21 Sep 56	
Blame It on My Youth	21 Sep 56	
What Is There to Say	21 Sep 56	
Sometimes I'm Happy	24 Sep 56	
I Know That You Know	24 Sep 56	
When I Grow Too Old to Dream	24 Sep 56	SM 131
Two Loves Have I	24 Sep 56	
True Blue Low	4 Oct 56	
Like Someone in Love	4 Oct 56	
I'm Shootin' High	4 Oct 56	
Tangerine	4 Oct 56	

One Sun	10 Oct 56		ST 2759
Maybe It's Because I Love You	19 Dec 56		
Love Letters	19 Dec 56		ST 21687
I Thought About Marie	19 Dec 56		SLCT 6129
Where Can I Go Without You?	19 Dec 56	EAP 1-824	SLCT 6129
Stardust	19 Dec 56		SLCT 6129/ST 21687/ SW3-1613
Love is the Thing	19 Dec 56	EAP 1-824	SLCT 6129
It's All in the Game	19 Dec 56		SLCT 6129/ST 21687
When I Fall in Love	28 Dec 56	EAP 1-824	SLCT 6129/SW 20664/ ST 21139
Ain't Misbehavin'	28 Dec 56		SLCT 6129/SM 133
When Sunny Gets Blue	28 Dec 56		SLCT 6129/SM 133
At Last	28 Dec 56		SLCT 6129/SM 133
Stay as Sweet as You Are	28 Dec 56	EAP 1-824	SLCT 6129/ST 21687
When Rock and Roll Came to Trinidad	19 Mar 57		
China Gate	19 Mar 57		SRS 5010
Blue Moon	14 May 57		
With You on My Mind	14 May 57		
Don't Try	14 May 57		
Send for Me	14 May 57		
Let's Make More Love	14 May 57		
Don't Get Around Much Anymore	10 Jul 57		SM 134
You'll Never Know	10 Jul 57		
The Song Is Ended	10 July 57		
Who's Sorry Now?	19 Jul 57		SM 133
The Foolish Things	19 Jul 57		SM 136
Once in a While	19 Jul 57		SM 134
The Song of Raintree County	19 Jul 57		SRS SP 509
Just One of Those Things	31 Jul 57		
I Should Care	31 Jul 57		
The Party's Over	31 Jul 57		ST 21687
Just for the Fun of It (remake of session 6133)	31 Jul 57		
A Cottage for Sale	7 Aug 57		
I Understand	7 Aug 57		
When Your Lover Has Gone	7 Aug 57		
There's a Gold Mine in the Sky	8 Aug 57		ST 2558
Around the World	8 Aug 57		ST 2558/ST 21687
An Affair to Remember	8 Aug 57		ST 2558/SM 132
Fascination	8 Aug 57		ST 2558

How Did I Change?	20 Nov 57	
Angel Smile	22 Nov 57	
It's None of My Affair	22 Nov 57	
Nothin' in the World	22 Nov 57	
Toys for Tots	22 Nov 57	
Beale Street Blues	29 Jan 58	MFP 1277
Yellow Dog Blues	29 Jan 58	MFP 1277
Careless Love	29 Jan 58	MFP 1277
Chantez Les Bas	29 Jan 58	MFP 1277
Overture a. Love Theme		
b. Hesitating Blues	30 Jan 58	MFP 1277
Morning Star	30 Jan 58	MFP 1277
Stay	30 Jan 58	MFP 1277
St. Louis Blues	30 Jan 58	SW3-1613-/MFP 1277
Harlem Blues	31 Jan 58	MFP 1277
Joe Turner's Blues	31 Jan 58	MFP 1277
Memphis Blues	31 Jan 58	MFP 1277
Friendless Blues	31 Jan 58	MFP 1277
Looking Back	4 Feb 58	
Make It Last	4 Feb 58	
Just as Much as Ever	4 Feb 58	
Thank You, Pretty		
Baby	1 Feb 58	ST 2759
Do I Like It?	4 Feb 58	
Maria Elena	17 Feb 58	
Lisbon Antigua	17 Feb 58	
Acércate Mas	17 Feb 58	
Tu, Mi Delirio	18 Feb 58	
Mardi Gras	18 Feb 58	
El Bodeguero Cha Cha		
Cha	18 Feb 58	
Magic Is the Moonlight	20 Feb 58	
Arrivederci Roma	20 Feb 58	SRS 5010/ST 21687
Quisas, Quisas, Quisas	20 Feb 58	
Los Mañanitas	20 Feb 58	
Adelita	20 Feb 58	
I Wish I Knew	2 May 58	SLCT 6173
This Is All I Ask	2 May 58	SLCT 6173
The More I See You	2 May 58	SLCT 6173
I Found a Million		
Dollar Baby	2 May 58	SLCT 6173
Making Believe		
You're Here	2 May 58	SLCT 6173
My Heart Tells Me	2 May 58	SLCT 6173
Cherchez La Femme	6 May 58	SLCT 6173
Don't Blame Me	6 May 58	
The Very Thought of You	6 May 58	SLCT 6173/ST 21687
No Greater Love	6 May 58	

Paradise	6 May 58	SLCT 6173/ SW 3-1613
Magnificent Obsession	8 May 58	SLCT 6173/SM 134
Cherie	8 May 58	SLCT 6173
Impossible	8 May 58	SLCT 6173
But Beautiful	8 May 58	SLCT 6173
For All We Know	8 May 58	SLCT 6173/ SRS SP 509
Chachito	9 Jun 58	
El Bodeguero	9 Jun 58	
Noche de Ronda	9 Jun 58	
Too Much	20 Jun 58	
I Got Love	20 Jun 58	
Lovesville	20 Jun 58	
Can't Help It	20 Jun 58	
Acérate Mas (Come Closer to Me)	30 Jun 58	MFP 5201
The Blues Don't Care	30 Jun 58	
Anytime, Anyway, Anywhere	30 Jun 58	
I Want a Little Girl	30 Jun 58	
Mood Indigo	30 Jun 58	
She's Funny That Way	30 Jun 58	
Avalon	1 Jul 58	
Baby, Won't You Please Come Home?	1 Jul 58	
The Late, Late Show	1 Jul 58	
Welcome to the Club	1 Jul 58	
Look Out for Love	2 Jul 58	
Wee Baby Blues	2 Jul 58	
Madrid	2 Jul 58	
To Whom It May Concern	11 Aug 58	
Love-Wise	11 Aug 58	
In the Heart of Jane Doe	11 Aug 58	
My Heart's Treasure	11 Aug 58	
You're Bringing Out the Dreamer in Me	11 Aug 58	
Bend a Little My Way	18 Aug 58	ST 2820
Non Dimenticar	18 Aug 58	
Coo Coo Roo Coo Coo Paloma	18 Aug 58	
Give Me Your Love	18 Aug 58	
This Morning It Was Summer	18 Aug 58	
A Thousand Thoughts of You	18 Aug 58	

Ain't Gonna Study War No More	29 Sep 58	
Everytime I Feel the Spirit	29 Sep 58	
Standin' in the Need of Prayer	29 Sep 58	
Go Down Moses	29 Sep 58	
Steal Away	29 Sep 58	
I Couldn't Hear Nobody Pray	30 Sep 58	
I Want to Be Ready	30 Sep 58	
Nobody Knows the Trouble I've Seen	30 Sep 58	
In the Sweet By and By	30 Sep 58	
Sweet Hour of Prayer	30 Sep 58	
Oh Mary Don't You Weep	30 Sep 58	SW 3-1613/SM 135
I Found the Answer	30 Sep 58	
For You	30 Oct 58	
Crazy She Calls Me	30 Oct 58	
Until the Real Thing Comes Along	30 Oct 58	SRS SP 509
You Are My Love	30 Oct 58	
The Best Thing for You Would Be Me	4 Nov 58	
Dedicated to You	4 Nov 58	
I Would Do Anything for You	4 Nov 58	
This Is Always	4 Nov 58	
I Had the Craziest Dream	5 Nov 58	ST 2558
I Wish I Knew	5 Nov 58	ST 2558
Be Still My Heart	5 Nov 58	ST 2558
As Far As I'm Concerned	7 Nov 58	SM 135
Lorelei	7 Nov 58	
This Holy Love	7 Nov 58	
You Made Me Love You	7 Nov 58	ST 2759
Peace of Mind	7 Nov 58	
Tell Me All About Yourself	10 Nov 58	SM 131
Dedicated to You	10 Nov 58	
When You Walked By	10 Nov 58	
You've Got the Indian Sign on Me	10 Nov 58	
My Life	10 Nov 58	
If You Said No	11 Nov 58	
Sweethearts on Parade	11 Nov 58	SRS SP 509
That's You	11 Nov 58	
When You Belong to Me	11 Nov 58	

Something Happens to Me	11 Nov 58	
Unfair	12 Nov 58	ST 2759
You're My Thrill	12 Nov 58	ST 2558
Again	12 Nov 58	SM 135
Laughable	12 Nov 58	
I Must Be Dreaming	12 Nov 58	
For the Want of a Kiss	12 Nov 58	ST 2558
The Night of the Quarter Moon	4 Feb 59	
Perfidia	14 Apr 59	SW 1220
Nádie Me Ama	14 Apr 59	SW 1220
Aquellos Ojos Verdes	14 Apr 59	SW 1220
Fantastico	14 Apr 59	SW 1220
El Choclo	14 Apr 59	SW 1220
Suas Maos	14 Apr 59	SW 1220
Capullito De Alelí	14 Apr 59	SW 1220
Come to the Mardi Gras	14 Apr 59	SW 1220
Cabaclo Do Rio	14 Apr 59	SW 1220
Ay Cosita Linda	14 Apr 59	SW 1220/SW 3-1613
Ansiedad	14 Apr 59	SW 1220
Yo Vendo Unos Ojos Negros	14 Apr 59	SW 1220
Brazilian Love Song	14 Apr 59	ST 2759/SRS 5010
Midnight Flyer	2 Jul 59	
Sweet Bird of Youth	2 Jul 59	
Buon Natale means (Merry Xmas to You)	2 Jul 59	
The Happiest Christmas Tree	2 Jul 59	
World in My Arms	2 Sep 59	
In a Mellow Tone	2 Sep 59	
Time and the River	2 Sep 59	
Whatcha Gonna Do	2 Sep 59	
(Remote-Vegas) Side 1	14 Jan 60	
(Remote-Vegas) Side 2	14 Jan 60	
Wild Is Love	1 Mar 60	CL 15358 SW 3-1613/SM 136
Hundreds and Thousands of Girls	1 Mar 60	
Tell Her in the Morning	1 Mar 60	
Pickup	1 Mar 60	
Stay with It	1 Mar 60	
Beggar for the Blues	1 Mar 60	
Wild Is Love (reprise)	1 Mar 60	
It's a Beautiful Evening	2 Mar 60	
World of No Return	2 Mar 60	
In Love Again	2 Mar 60	
Wouldn't You Know	2 Mar 60	

Are You Disenchanted?	2 Mar 60	
He Who Hesitates	2 Mar 60	
Steady	9 Mar 60	
My Love	9 Mar 60	
Is It Better to Have Loved and Lost?	9 Mar 60	
Wild Is Love (Opening)	9 Mar 60	SW 3-1613
When It's Summer	9 Mar 60	ST 2820
Magic Night	9 Mar 60	ST 2759
Someone to Tell It To	11 Mar 60	
Baby Blue	11 Mar 60	
You Are Mine	11 Mar 60	
Away in a Manger	5 Jul 60	SW 1444
I Saw Three Ships	5 Jul 60	SW 1444
Silent Night	5 Jul 60	SW 1444
The First Noel	5 Jul 60	SW 1444
Joy to the World	6 Jul 60	SW 1444
Deck the Halls	6 Jul 60	SW 1444
Hark the Herald Angels Sing	6 Jul 60	SW 1444
O Come All Ye Faithful	6 Jul 60	SW 1444
O Tannenbaum	6 Jul 60	SW 1444
A Cradle in Bethlehem	7 Jul 60	SW 1444
God Rest Ye Merry Gentlemen	7 Jul 60	SW 1444
Caroling Caroling	7 Jul 60	SW 1444
O Holy Night	7 Jul 60	SW 1444
O Little Town of Bethlehem	7 Jul 60	SW 1444
If I Knew	27 Sep 60	ST 2820
The Touch of Your Lips	23 Dec 60	SRS SP 509
You're Mine You	23 Dec 60	SM 132
Illusion	23 Dec 60	
Funny	23 Dec 60	SRS SP 509/SM 132
Not So Long Ago	23 Dec 60	
Only Forever	23 Dec 60	
Lights Out	23 Dec 60	SM 131
I Remember You	22 Dec 60	SRS SP 509/SM 136
Sunday, Monday or Always	22 Dec 60	
A Nightingale Sang in Berkeley Square	22 Dec 60	SRS 5010/SM 136
My Need for You	22 Dec 60	
Poinciana	22 Dec 60	SRS SP 509
It's Only a Paper Moon	22 Mar 61	SW 1-1613/ SW 20664
Sweet Lorraine	22 Mar 61	SW 1-1613/SW 20664/ ST 21139

Straighten Up and Fly Right	23 Mar 61		SW 1-1613/SW 20664/ SM 133
Embraceable You	23 Mar 61		
Route 66	23 Mar 61		SW 1-1613/SW 20664/ ST 21139/SM 132
For Sentimental Reasons	23 Mar 61		SW 1-1613
Answer Me My Love	24 Mar 61	CL 15588	SW 2-1613/ST 21139/ SM 134
Darling, Je Vous Aime Beaucoup	24 Mar 61		SW 2-1613/SRS 5010
Smile	24 Mar 61		SW 2-1613/ST 21687/ SM 135
Pretend	24 Mar 61		SW 2-1613
Sand and the Sea	27 Mar 61		SW 2-1613
A Blossom Fell	27 Mar 61		SW 2-1613/SM 132
Nature Boy	27 Mar 61	EAP 20053	SW 1-1613/SW 20664/ ST 21687
Too Young	29 Mar 61		SW 1-1613/SW 20664/ ST 21139
Somewhere Along the Way	29 Mar 61		SW 1-1613/SW 20664/ ST 21687
Unforgettable	30 Mar 61	EAP 20053	SW 2-1613/SW 20664/ ST 21139/SM 136
Mona Lisa	30 Mar 61	EAP 20053	SW 1-1613/SW 20664/ ST 21139/SM 135
The Christmas Song	30 Mar 61		SW 1-1613/SM 132
Goodnight Little Leaguer	4 Apr 61		
Because You Love Me	4 Apr 61		
Take a Fool's Advice	4 Apr 61		
The First Baseball Game	4 Apr 61		
Make It Last	4 Apr 61		ST 2759
Send for Me	3 Apr 61		SW 3-1613
If I May	3 Apr 61		SW 2-1613
Looking Back	3 Apr 61		SW 3-1613
Capuccina	7 Apr 61		
Let True Love Begin	7 Apr 61		SRS SP 509
Love	7 Apr 61		
I Heard You Cried Last Night	7 Apr 61		
Orange Colored Sky	6 Jul 61		SW 1-1613/SW 20664
To the Ends of the Earth	19 Jul 61		SW 3-1613/SRS 5010
Non Dimenticar	19 Jul 61		SW 3-1613/ST 21687/ ST 1659
Blue Gardenia	19 Jul 61		SW 2-1613/SRS 5039
Night Lights	19 Jul 61		SW 3-1613
Calypso Blues	19 Jul 61		SW 1-1613/SRS 5010
Walkin' My Baby Back Home	19 Jul 61	EAP 20053	SW 2-1613/ST 21139

I Am in Love	20 Jul 61		SW 2-1613/SRS 5039
Lush Life	20 Jul 61		SW 1-1613
Ballerina	20 Jul 61		SW 3-1613/SW 20664
Ebony Rhapsody	20 Nov 61		
Day In, Day Out	20 Nov 61		SRS SP 509
Too Little Too Late	20 Nov 61		
When My Sugar Walks Down the Street	20 Nov 61		SRS SP 509/ SW 20664/SM 133
Cold Cold Heart	21 Nov 61		SRS SP 509
Let's Face the Music and Dance	21 Nov 61		SRS SP 509
Something Makes Me Want to Dance	21 Nov 61		
I'm Gonna Sit Right Down and Write Myself a Letter	21 Nov 61		SRS SP 509
Rules of the Road	22 Nov 61		
Warm and Willing	22 Nov 61		SRS SP 509
Bidin' My Time	22 Nov 61		SRS SP 509
Moon Love	22 Nov 61		SM 131
Step Right Up	27 Nov 61		
Magic Moments	27 Nov 61		ST 2759
The Right Thing to Say	27 Nov 61		
Azure-Te	19 Dec 61		SW 1675
Everything Happens to Me	19 Dec 61		
A Beautiful Friendship	19 Dec 61	CL 15588	SW 1675
Pick Yourself Up	20 Dec 61		SW 1675
September Song	20 Dec 61		SW 1675
Let There Be Love	20 Dec 61		SW 1675/SW 20664/ ST 21139
I Got It Bad	20 Dec 61		SW 1675
Serenata	20 Dec 61		SW 1675
In Other Words (Fly Me to the Moon)	20 Dec 61		SW 1675
The Game of Love	21 Dec 61		
Guess I'll Go Back Home	21 Dec 61		
I'm Lost	22 Dec 61		SW 1675
Don't Go	22 Dec 61		SW 1675
There's a Lull in My Life	22 Dec 61		SW 1675
Lost April	22 Dec 61		SW 1675
Look No Further	7 Feb 62		
La Féria de Las Flores	6 Mar 62		
Guadalajara	6 Mar 62		
Las Golondrinas	6 Mar 62		SRS 5010
Tres Palabras (Without You)	7 Mar 62		
Piel Canela	7 Mar 62		
Solamente Una Vez	7 Mar 62		

Chiapanecas	8 Mar 62	
Vaya Condios	8 Mar 62	
Adios Mariquita Linda	9 Mar 62	
No Me Platiques	9 Mar 62	
Aqui Se Habla Amor	9 Mar 62	
A Média Luz	9 Mar 62	
Dear Lonely Hearts	19 Jun 62	ST 21139
Ramblin' Rose	19 Jun 62	ST 21139/SW 20664/
		ST 1793/SM 131
Nothing Goes Up	19 Jun 62	
The Good Times	19 Jun 62	ST 1793
Who's Next in Line?	19 Jun 62	
When You're Smiling	11 Aug 62	ST 1793/SM 133
Wolverton Mountain	11 Aug 62	ST 1793
One Has My Name, the Other Has My Heart	11 Aug 62	ST 1793
Skip to My Lou	11 Aug 62	ST 1793
Sing Another Song	11 Aug 62	ST 1793
Your Cheatin' Heart	11 Aug 62	ST 1793
Goodnight Irene	11 Aug 62	ST 1793
I Don't Want It That Way	11 Aug 62	ST 1793
Twilight on the Trail	11 Aug 62	ST 1793
He'll Have to Go	11 Aug 62	ST 1793
Farewell to Arms	13 Aug 62	ST 2558
Happy New Year	13 Aug 62	ST 2558
When the World Was Young	13 Aug 62	SRS SP 509
Spring Is Here	13 Aug 62	
I Don't Want Her	13 Aug 62	
Say It Isn't So	13 Aug 62	SRS SP 509
Am I Blue	13 Aug 62	
Laughing on the Outside	14 Aug 62	W/SW 1859
Back to Joe's	14 Aug 62	
The End of a Love Affair	14 Aug 62	
That's All There Is	14 Aug 62	
Someone To Tell It To	14 Aug 62	
If Love Ain't There	14 Aug 62	
Where Did Everyone Go?	14 Aug 62	
Miss You	12 Nov 62	
Oh, How I Miss You Tonight	12 Nov 62	
All Over the World	12 Nov 62	
Lonesome and Sorry	12 Nov 62	
My First and Only Lover	12 Nov 62	
Near You	13 Nov 62	
Why Should I Cry Over You?	13 Nov 62	
Yearning	13 Nov 62	
All By Myself	13 Nov 62	

It's a Lonesome Old Town	13 Nov 62		SM 134
Misery Loves Company	13 Nov 62		
In the Cool of the Day	11 Apr 63		
Those Lazy Hazy Crazy Days of Summer	11 Apr 63		ST 1932/ST 21139/ SM 131
Felicia	11 Apr 63		ST 2820
You'll See	11 Apr 63		ST 2820
Mr. Wishing Well	11 Apr 63		
On the Sidewalks of New York	15 May 63		ST 1932/SRS 5010
Get Out and Get Under the Moon	15 May 63		ST 1932
After the Ball Is Over	15 May 63		ST 1932
There Is a Tavern in the Town	15 May 63		ST 1932
On a Bicycle Built for Two (Daisybell)	15 May 63		ST 1932
In the Good Old Summertime	15 May 63		ST 1932
That Sunday, That Summer	16 May 63		ST 1932/SRS SP 509/ SM 134
Our Old Home Team	16 May 63		ST 1932
Don't Forget	16 May 63		ST 1932
You Tell Me Your Dream	16 May 63		ST 1932
That's What They Meant	16 May 63		ST 1932
Wouldn't It Be Loverly?	17 Sep 63		
I've Grown Accustomed to Her Face	17 Sep 63		SRS SP 509
I Could Have Danced All Night	17 Sep 63		
With a Little Bit of Luck	18 Sep 63		SRS SP 509/SW 20664
You Did It	18 Sep 63		
Show Me	18 Sep 63		
I'm an Ordinary Man	19 Sep 63		
Hymn to Him	19 Sep 63		
Get Me to the Church on Time	19 Sep 63		SRS SP 509
Rain in Spain	20 Sep 63		
On the Street Where You Live	20 Sep 63		SRS SP 509
Silver Bird	14 Jan 64		
My True Carrie, Love	14 Jan 64		
I Don't Want to Be Hurt Anymore	14 Jan 64		ST 21139
A Rag, a Bone, a Hank of Hair	14 Jan 64		
People	14 Jan 64	CL 15358	SRS 5039/ST 2795
Let Me Tell You	14 Jan 64		

Go If You're Going	5 May 64	
I'm Alone Because I Love You	5 May 64	SRS SP 509
Don't You Remember	5 May 64	
I'm All Cried Out	5 May 64	
I Don't Want to See Tomorrow	5 May 64	SRS SP 509
You're My Everything	5 May 64	SRS SP 509/SW 20664
Brush Those Tears from Your Eyes	27 May 64	SRS SP 509
You're Crying on My Shoulder	27 May 64	
Was That the Human Thing to Do?	27 May 64	SRS SP 509
Only Yesterday	27 May 64	SM 131
Road to Nowhere	27 May 64	
Love	3 Jun 64	ST 21139
Wanderlust	3 Jun 64	
Marnie	3 Jun 64	ST 2820
More and More of Your Amore	3 Jun 64	
Love—Italian	18 Aug 64	
I Don't Want to Be Hurt Anymore—Japanese	26 Aug 64	
Le Bonheur C'est Quand on S'aime	26 Aug 64	
You'll See	26 Aug 64	ST 2820
Autumn Leaves—Japanese	27 Aug 64	
Autumn Leaves—French	27 Aug 64	
Tu Eres Tan Amable —Spanish	27 Aug 64	
Tu Sei Cosi Amabile —Italian	27 Aug 64	
More	1 Dec 64	
How I'd Love to Love You	1 Dec 64	
Coquette	1 Dec 64	SRS SP 509
My Kind of Girl	2 Dec 64	SRS SP 509
More	2 Dec 64	SRS SP 509
Your Love	2 Dec 64	
Thanks to You	2 Dec 64	SRS SP 509
There's Love	2 Dec 64	
Swiss Retreat	2 Dec 64	
The Girl from Ipanema	3 Dec 64	SRS 5010
Three Little Words	3 Dec 64	SRS SP 509
No Other Heart	3 Dec 64	SM 131
The Ballad of Cat Ballou w/Stubby Kay		SRS SP 509
They Can't Make Her Cry		SRS SP 509